M000250863

Ancestral Roots of the Jats

DNA Revelations

David G. Mahal

Published by DGM Associates
PO Box 1146
Pacific Palisades, CA 90272

ISBN-13: 978-0692369593 (DGM Associates)
ISBN-10: 0692369597

Library of Congress Control Number: 2015900839
DGM Associates, Pacific Palisades, CA

Printed by CreateSpace, an Amazon.com Company
North Charleston, SC

Printed in the United States of America

Available from Amazon.com and other retail outlets
Available on Kindle and other devices

To my parents and ancestors.

Contents

PREFACE

> It is the traveler from an antique land who lives within us all.
> — Bryan Sykes

The Jats represent an ethnic community that has inhabited the northwest region of the Indian subcontinent for several thousand years. This book is about the ancient origins of the Jat people, going back long before history was recorded in written language. The following exploration is a personal quest for me because I happen to be from this community.

My grandfather wrote a book about the antiquity of the Jats.[1] Since his book was published in 1955, historians and academics have published more books about the Jat people. The conclusion in practically all of these books is similar: the Jat people are descendants of Aryans, Indo-Scythians, Medes, or other nomadic groups who arrived and lived in a large part of northern India at one time. Some writers say the Jats originated from Jutland in Scandinavia.

The evidence tends to be anecdotal or superficial, such as the similarity of certain words of the language and comparisons of some habits and social customs. For example, because the Scythians smoked marijuana and this practice prevails in some Jat villages, a connection between the two is inferred. But that does not constitute hard evidence. Marijuana has been used in many parts of the world for thousands of years.

Historical discrepancies remain regarding when these people arrived and whether they were peaceful or violent. There tends to be a replication of what others have written. Most writers have said more or less the same thing in different words.

Considering the great diversity of people in India and the differences in physiognomy among the Jat community, I have always been skeptical of assertions that the Jats are descendants of any single group of people. In his book about the antiquity of Jats, my grandfather wrote, "This brief work is meant chiefly to excite the ambition of interested research worker[s]..." I think he would approve of the approach I have taken, using scientific and other knowledge that did not exist during his time. Essentially, this book updates what he wrote sixty years ago. It explains the ancestral roots of the Jat people through the lens of DNA science, correcting and confirming aspects of their history as handed down through the generations or as theorized by those who lacked those tools.

The basic conclusion is that the Jat community does not have a pure ancestral line. They share their lineages with many other ethnic communities in the Indian subcontinent. Based on my research, I describe the six major ancestral groups of Jats in detail, along with their geographical origins, and identify other major ethnic communities in the

Indian subcontinent that have the same genetic origins as the Jats.

It must be noted that in studying ancestry, many scientific techniques, such as DNA analysis, were not available until recently. This book provides a startling reassessment of Jat ancestry and revises what has been written in history books for many years. It is inappropriate to continue to generalize all Jats as descendants of a specific group of people, such as the Aryans, Scythians, Medes, or Scandinavians. It is my hope that the new findings, which are based on DNA science and presented in this book, are provocative enough to start a much-needed discussion and clarify the subject once and for all.

David G. Mahal
Los Angeles, California
March 2015

INTRODUCTION

> In all of us there is a hunger, marrow-deep,
> to know our heritage – to know who we are
> and where we have come from.
> – Alex Haley

The Jats are traditionally an agricultural society, although during the last few hundred years, many of them have moved on to other diverse professions and fields, including business, academia, medicine, and politics. Jats occupy many prominent positions, both in India and other countries.

A few thousand years ago, the Jats initially adopted Hinduism as their religion. Later, some of them likely became Buddhists and Jains. After Islam reached north India around the eleventh century, a number of people in the area converted to this new religion. Later, during various Muslim invasions, more people converted to Islam fearing the "sword of Islam," as some invaders called it. After Sikhism was founded in the fifteenth century, some Hindu and Muslim Jats converted to this new religion. It is only during the last one thousand years that the Jats have separated into three distinct, religion-based communities—Hindus, Muslims, and Sikhs. Many Jats, irrespective of their religion, still share the same family names.

According to the Census of India, the last time the population was surveyed based on caste, in 1931, there were about ten million Jats. They belonged to their three main religions as follows.[1]

- Hinduism—47 percent
- Islam—33 percent
- Sikhism—20 percent

Since the partition of India in 1947, Sikh and Hindu Jats have lived primarily in India, in the states of Delhi, Haryana, Punjab, Rajasthan, and Uttar Pradesh. The main languages spoken are Hindustani, Haryanvi, and Punjabi. The Muslim

Jats have lived primarily in Pakistan, in the provinces of Balochistan, Northwest Frontier, Punjab, and Sindh. Depending on where they live, the main languages spoken are Balochi, Punjabi, Sindhi, and Urdu. Many Jats have migrated overseas, and they can be found in all corners of the world, including Australia, Canada, England, New Zealand, and the United States.

In 2012, the *Hindustan Times* reported the Jat population in India was about 82,500,000.[2] Assuming the 1931 ratio among religions has stayed about the same (i.e., 33 percent for Islam and 67 percent combined for Hinduism and Sikhism), the extrapolated population of Muslim Jats in 2012 is estimated to be about 40,600,000 (82,500,000/67 x 33). On this basis, the total population of all Hindu, Muslim, and Sikh Jats in India and Pakistan is estimated to be around 123 million people. That number is roughly equal to the total population of France, Spain, and Portugal. In short, in only eighty-one years—from 1931 to 2012—the Jats have propagated into a very large community on this planet.

Origins of the Jats

My previous book, *Before India: Exploring Your Ancestry with DNA*, covered the ancient origins of fifty-two key ethnic communities of the Indian subcontinent, along with several people of Indian and Pakistani origin living in some other countries.[3] This is a shorter version of that book and focuses on only one ethnic community. I have extracted and summarized from the original book whatever information is specifically applicable to the Jat community and rearranged it in two parts.

Part One—The People

This section explains that written history is a recent development for humans and goes back less than 2500 years. Using archeological and other evidence, it describes the people who came to India starting about a hundred thousand years ago and eventually populated the subcontinent.

I provide a thumbnail sketch of Indian history, reviewing more recent migrations and invasions that occurred over the last thirty thousand years. The migrants intermixed with local populations, and as a result, India today is a colorful tapestry of hundreds of ethnic groups with distinct cultures and languages. As explained in a later part of the book, the ancestry of these people goes to many corners of this planet.

Part Two—DNA Roots

In this part, I briefly explain the science of genes and genealogy. The section describes the Human Genome Project (HGP), which was completed in 2000 and surveyed the genetic design of the human being. It contains explanations of genes and how DNA analysis is used to trace ancestry.

This section also explains my study of the DNA results of 1,291 individuals in fifty-two ethnic communities in the Indian subcontinent, as covered in my earlier book, *Before India: Exploring Your Ancestry with DNA*. As a part of this study, a combined sample of Jat Sikhs and Haryana Jats is used to determine their origins. The results of this study identified six major ancestral groups for this population. They are described in more detail in the following pages.

Part One
The People

This section demonstrates why written history is not always accurate. It explains how India was populated, starting about a hundred thousand years ago, and describes the origins of modern humans and the first migrations out of Africa. It also provides a thumbnail sketch of Indian history and summary of some of the most recent migrations and invasions to illustrate the diversity of this region's people, who came from different corners of the planet, settled in India, and intermixed with populations that had arrived earlier.

Chapter 1
The Written Word

> History will be kind to me, for I intend to write it.
> —Winston Churchill

There are two major avenues to better understand the past: archaeology and written texts. Although archaeologists have excavated objects that are millions of years old, there are no written records of ancient history. Written language is a recent development, and history books go back only so far.

Origins of Language

It is generally agreed that humans started speaking languages only about one hundred thousand years ago. But the earliest written language, known as the cuneiform system of writing, was invented in Mesopotamia (Sumer, present Iraq) much later, around 3200 BCE. We need to remember that in the long history of humankind, the first *written* language was developed only about five thousand years ago.

The earliest form of Sanskrit, known as Vedic Sanskrit, goes back to about 1700 BCE. The Tamil language in South India has a literature going back to about the same time. The Rig Veda, the oldest of the sacred books of Hinduism, was composed about 1500 BCE and preserved orally until it was written down about 300 BCE.

The Mahabharata, an epic poem of ancient India, serves as an important source of information about Hinduism between 400 BCE and 200 CE. The Ramayana is another epic poem of India; it was composed around 300 BCE. But there is no definitive written record of the history of India before Alexander the Great's invasion in 326 BCE. The written history of India we have is less than 2400 years old.

HISTORY OF JATS

There is an abundance of books written about the history of the Jats. At my last count, the total was at least thirty books and writings, not including articles in newspapers and magazines. Colonel James Tod, an officer of the East India Company and an Oriental scholar, was one of the first to write about Jats in 1829. Many scholars and writers have followed suit. The conclusion in practically all of these books is similar and repetitive: the Jat people are descendants of Aryans, Indo-Scythians, Medes, or other similar groups who arrived and lived in a large part of northern India.

A few historians even say that Aryans and Scythians are the same people. It is also written that the Aryan migrations to India started around 1500 BCE, and the Scythians arrived much later, around 110 BCE. There are discrepancies, and the historical debates continue.

There is even controversy about the origin of the

Aryans. A recent study by Indian geneticists from the Centre for Cellular and Molecular Biology (CCMB) in Hyderabad reported that the widely believed theory of Aryan invasions is a myth. "Our study clearly shows that there was no genetic influx 3,500 years ago," said Dr. Kumarasamy Thangaraj of CCMB. He led the research team that included scientists from the University of Tartu, Chettinad Academy of Research and Education in Chennai, and Banaras Hindu University (BHU). "It is high time we re-write India's prehistory based on scientific evidence," said Dr. Lalji Singh, former director of CCMB, former vice chancellor of Banaras Hindu University, and coauthor of the study. "There is no genetic evidence that Indo-Aryans invaded or migrated to India or even something such as Aryans existed."[1]

Historians are prone to chronicling events and episodes. They tend to quote each other, and the first person who writes something unique is referenced repeatedly by others, often without any verification of what was written. Right or wrong, history tends to perpetuate itself and the same things get written over and over. But the historian's primary responsibility is to provide reliable narratives. Since the nineteenth century, academics and historians have paid careful attention to how sources are chosen and interpreted.[2] However, this has not been the case with all historians, even those of considerable repute.

Documenting History

The Romans and Greeks were the first to take a formal interest in writing down history. Let us consider Herodotus, a Greek historian, who is used as a source of information in several books and writings about ancient India. Many Indian historians have relied considerably on what he wrote. He was a storyteller who lived from 484 to 425 BCE in modern-day Turkey. He produced one lengthy book, *The Histories,* which has been translated and divided into nine volumes.[3] For Herodotus, history meant *inquiry*, and his writings are devoted not only to the past but also to geography, ethnology, and myth. There is no evidence that he visited India.

Herodotus wrote about the Callatiae and Padaei people of India, who apparently killed their elders when they became sick or old and feasted on their bodies. He wrote that Indian tribes copulated in the open like cattle, and men had black semen, like the color of their skins. He wrote about giant ants in India that were bigger than a fox, though not so big as a dog. He was confused about geography and thought India existed toward the south of Persia. It is believed that he wrote his accounts around 440 BCE.

In depicting the Indians as savages, it is obvious that Herodotus was ignorant of the highly developed civilization that existed in India before and during his time. For instance, Mehrgarh was established in northern India about 6,500 years before his writings, and the Indus Valley Civilization existed until about one thousand years before his time.

There are enough archaeological excavations to show that even several thousand years before Herodotus's time, Indians buried their dead in the Indus Valley and did not engage in the funerary cannibalism practices he wrote about. As an example, Mohenjo Daro is a major settlement of the Indus civilization. The name means "mound of the dead," and it contains many burial sites.

Apparently, Herodotus was unaware of the existence of Hinduism in India. Mahavira founded Jainism and Gautama Buddha Buddhism in India long before Herodotus's writings. By about 700 BCE, long before the universities of Oxford, Cambridge, and Bologna were established, the world's first major center of higher learning was founded in Taxila, with students from all parts of

India and some adjoining countries.[4] Although Darius the Great annexed Taxila to the Achaemenid Persian Empire around 500 BCE, apparently Herodotus was unaware of this seat of higher learning across the border.

Scholars of his time had different opinions about him. Cicero called Herodotus the "father of history,"[5] yet the Greek writer Plutarch, in his *Moralia* (Ethics), dubbed Herodotus the "father of lies."[6] Plutarch suggested that Herodotus's appeal lay in his flattering accounts of Greek exploits and accused him of deliberate falsehood. Herodotus's reputation as a liar did not end with Plutarch. Many other critics accused him of passing on the stories of his informants as history. Even Alexander the Great was aware that Herodotus's fanciful accounts of India were based on hearsay.[7]

Similarly, there are other ancient writers like Ptolemy, Megasthenes, Strabo, Ktesias (or Ctesias), and Pliny who have written something or other about India. Of these, Megasthenes was the only one who spent considerable time in India and wrote based on his personal observations. The others wrote what they heard secondhand through traders, sailors, Persian officers, and others who had visited India.

These examples are noteworthy, because many Indian and other historians seem to be in awe of Herodotus and other ancient writers and base their conclusions on their writings. We need to be cautious about the accuracy of historical information, whether it has been verified, and how it is interpreted and used. We should also remember that written history goes back less than 2500 years. Unless there is archaeological or scientific evidence to support what is written, ancient history needs to be reviewed with caution.

CHAPTER 2
FIRST ARRIVALS

> It is not the strongest or the most intelligent who will survive but those who can best manage change.
> —Charles Darwin

It is a basic drive among living creatures to move around and seek better environments for food and shelter. Birds, terrestrial animals, and water dwellers have done it since time immemorial. Storks and cranes from the cold regions of Russia and China make the treacherous journey over the Himalayas to India during the winter months. Canadian geese fly long distances to winter in the southerly, warmer parts of North America. Even fragile, dainty monarch butterflies migrate by the millions to the warmer climates of California and Mexico every winter. Many types of whales swim toward the colder poles in the summer and toward the more tropical waters of the equator in the winter. Humans have done the same thing and populated the entire planet rapidly. It is happening to this day; legally or illegally, every year, people migrate from less-developed areas to more developed ones for better opportunities. It all started in Africa.

2.1 Monarch butterflies

Emergence of Modern Humans

It is well established that modern humans evolved in Africa about two hundred thousand years ago and migrated to the rest of the world over the last one hundred thousand years. There are two competing hypotheses in paleoanthropology (the study of human beginnings) regarding the origins of *Homo sapiens* or modern humans. One states that they migrated out of Africa about one hundred thousand years ago and replaced older hominids (obligate bipedal primate mammals, including early humans) in Europe and Asia by about fifty thousand years ago. The other hypothesis states that modern humans evolved in different parts of the world but allows for contributions from Africa.

According to Dr. Luigi Cavalli-Sforza, a noted Stanford University scholar, "From a geneticist's point of view, a single origin followed by expansion is the more credible of the two."[1] Research supports the African-origin hypothesis. Scientists have compared 650,000 genetic markers in about a thousand individuals from fifty-one populations around the globe and concluded that modern humans gradually settled the world after leaving Africa.[2] Based on anatomical, archaeological, and genetic evidence, the current scientific explanation for the beginning of all modern humans is the model that claims an African origin.[3]

Out of Africa

We should note that the early humans were primitive people, just slightly ahead of the animals, searching for shelter in trees, caves, and huts. They walked into unknown territories and adapted to different climates. They lived on jungle produce or fish if they were close to water, and not all of them may have known how to make fire. They used sticks, stones, and bones to make tools and weapons.

Research suggests that some groups practiced incest until they learned that it led to different diseases and deformities. Some tribes, like those mentioned by Herodotus, engaged in cannibalism. They suffered natural calamities and encountered dangerous animals in their paths. Many perished because of diseases for which there were no cures.

The initial migrants traveled north and crossed into the Arabian Peninsula. Some traveled further north into Central Asia, which became the staging ground for migrations to Serbia and Europe. Others traveled as beachcombers along the southern coast of the Arabian Peninsula. They moved east toward India and continued to Indonesia, Borneo, China, and Australasia.

Our planet was advancing into an ice age, which made the continents bigger and joined them in certain places. Walking a coastal route to the Far East and Australia was easier than it would be today. Some people continued northeast toward Siberia. There was an ice bridge between Siberia and Alaska at that time, and about twenty thousand years ago, people crossed this bridge and populated North and South America. Scientists believe that this initial group may have been as small as twenty people.

The migration through India was interrupted about seventy-four thousand years ago by the eruption of Mount Toba in Sumatra, Indonesia. This was one of the largest volcanic eruptions in this planet's history. The catastrophe caused a six-year nuclear winter and a thousand-year ice age. North Atlantic surface temperatures and global sea levels dropped significantly. Volcanic ash up to twenty feet deep covered the Indian subcontinent, and the population of the region fell dramatically. As a result, the human population on the planet may have dropped to about two thousand people, and humans almost became extinct.[4]

Michael Petraglia and his team from the University of Cambridge discovered stone tools at a site called Jwalapuram in Andhra Pradesh, South India, above and below a thick layer of ash from the Toba eruption. This suggests that life continued for humans living in the area.[5]

A warming of the climate allowed repopulation of the area. New migrations out of Africa from about fifty thousand years ago populated India with large numbers of humans who later became known as Dravidians. Another reliable record of modern humans in the area was the recent discovery of the *Homo sapiens balangodensis* (Balangoda man) in Sri Lanka. The specimen has been dated to about thirty-seven thousand years ago.[6] This finding is consistent with other similar research from this period.

Since 2005, the National Geographic Society has conducted the Genographic Project to analyze and better understand historical patterns in human DNA from participants around the world. A study headed by Dr. Ramasamy Pitchappan of Chettinad University, who served as the regional director of Genographic India, found that people living in villages near Madurai in South India carried the same rare genetic markers as some Australian Aborigines and people living in Africa. The finding showed a link between the three continents and confirmed that the people in Australia and India who carried this genetic marker were likely descendants of the original migrants from Africa.[7]

The migrations out of Africa did not proceed in straight lines. After people settled an area, clans formed and then dispersed in different directions. The clans grew in size and clashed with each other for power and territorial rights. Some backtracked and returned to their original areas. Over thousands of years, populations increased everywhere. Improved tools and weapons were created, and wars broke out between people. Leaders emerged, and kingdoms and empires came into existence.

Although the migrations out of Africa to India and beyond initially proceeded along the coast, some migrants spread to the inner parts of the subcontinent. It is believed that the new migrants bred with the older *Homo erectus* species, as evidenced by the Narmada Man, which existed in India as long as three hundred thousand years ago. Waves of incursions into India continued over thousands of years, and people came from many different parts of the globe.

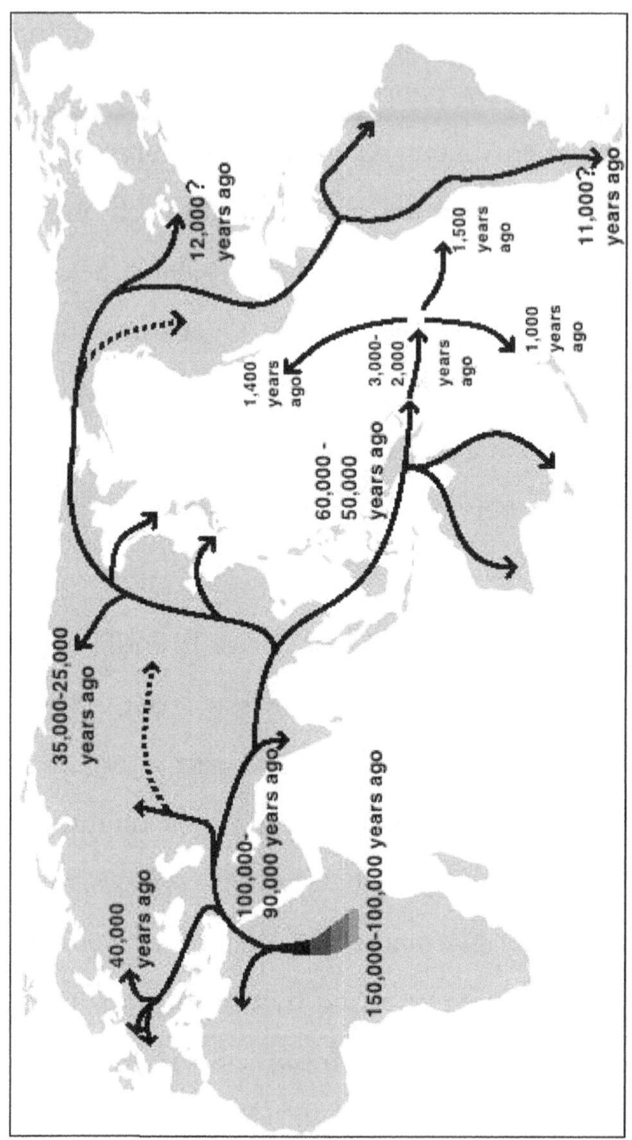

2.2. Initial migrations out of Africa
(Map: National Institute for Genetics, Japan)

Chapter 3
New Migrations

People will not look forward to posterity who never look backward to their ancestors.
—Edmund Burke

Many migrations were peaceful, and many were extremely violent, with massacres of large numbers of people who were already there. The arrivals multiplied and created a large population in India. A review of some of these key migrations and invasions will help us develop insights into the foreign influences and diverse groups that populated India.

We should keep in mind that peaceful migrations usually include families and children, but invaders normally do not travel with their wives and children. Many of them may not even have families. After killing the men opposing them, the winning marauders tended to take the local women and rape or marry them.

This has been the case during wars everywhere. Many invaders go back to where they came from, taking their loot with them, and others settle in the conquered area and create new families. In this manner, foreign and indigenous genes are mixed. The following pages deal only glancingly with Indian history; the purpose is to illustrate the diversity of people who came to this land. Only the period from about 30,000 BCE to the start of the Mughal Empire around 1500 CE is covered.

30,000 BCE: Bhimbetka Caves

In 1957–58, Indian archaeologist Dr. Vishnu Wakankar discovered prehistoric rock shelters in Bhimbetka near Bhopal in Madhya Pradesh. Named a World Heritage Site by the United Nations Educational, Scientific, and Cultural Organization (UNESCO), there are more than seven hundred rock shelters and hundreds of paintings carved in stone.

3.1 Bhimbetka rock art

Some of these shelters were inhabited by the Homo erectus species (premodern humans) more than three hundred thousand years ago.[1] Many other people lived in the shelters over the years. Although not fully corroborated, according to the Archaeological Survey of India, the name Bhimbetka is derived from Bhima (the second of the five Pandava brothers named in the Mahabharata) who stayed in the caves at one time.[2] The stone art is more than thirty thousand years old and among the oldest known rock art sites (the Chauvet Cave paintings in France go back thirty-seven thousand years, and the newly discovered El Castillo cave paintings in Spain are 40,800 years old).

The art was produced over a long period. The colors used are derived from vegetation. The art has endured over a long period of time because the drawings were made deep inside the caves. More recent artwork shows horses or similar animals and the riders holding what appear to be spears or weapons. The artwork suggests that domesticated horses and similar animals existed in the area in the distant past.

7000 BCE: Indus Valley Civilization

Also known as the Harappan Civilization, the Indus Valley Civilization arose in northwestern India. Major sites of this period include Mehrgarh, Harappa, Mohenjo Daro, Dholavira, Ganeriwala, Rakhigarhi, Rupar, and Lothal. Some sites are in current-day Pakistan, and some are in India. Originally, the Indus Valley Civilization was thought to have evolved around 3750 BCE, but research has pushed the origin of this civilization back several thousand years. At the International Conference on Harappan Archaeology held by the Archaeological Survey of India in Chandigarh in 2012, it was announced that on the basis of radiometric dates and excavations at sites in Pakistan and India, "the cultural remains of the pre-Harappan horizon go back to 7380 BC to 6201 BC."[3]

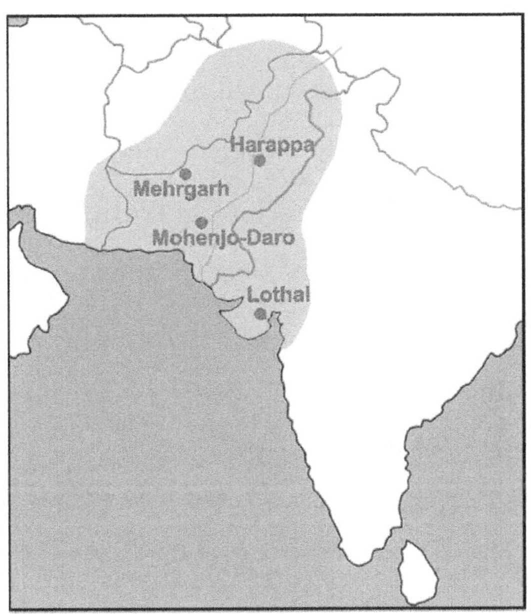

3.2 Indus Valley Civilization

Mehrgarh, another UNESCO World Heritage Site, lies in the Kachi Plain of Balochistan in Pakistan. The site was discovered in 1974 by French archaeologists Jean-François and Catherine Jarrige, and it is older than the pyramids of Giza. Mounds discovered in the area show that humans buried their dead thousands of years ago. The Jarriges also unearthed clay pots, ornaments, buildings, and other items.

The people of Mehrgarh lived in mud-brick houses, stored grain in granaries, fashioned tools with copper ore, and lined large basket containers with bitumen. They cultivated barley, einkorn, wheat, jujubes, and dates, and they herded sheep, goats, and cattle. Horse bones have been found in the ruins. These were probably the earliest agriculturists in South Asia.[4]

3.3 Indus Pottery

3.4 Meheraarh houses

The site was occupied until about 2600 BCE.[5] Residents directed their efforts into crafts, including tanning, bead production, and metalworking. There is evidence that the people had contact with cultures in northern Afghanistan, northeastern Iran, and south-central Asia and carried on commerce with Arabia.[6]

An advanced urban culture is evident in the Indus Valley Civilization. The quality of town layouts suggests knowledge of urban planning and a government that placed a high priority on hygiene.

Water was obtained from wells, some homes had a room set aside for bathing, and wastewater was directed to covered drains.

3.5 Mohenjo Daro

The people of this civilization were among the first to develop a system of uniform weights and measures. In 2001, archaeologists studying the remains of two men from Mehrgarh discovered a tradition of protodentistry in the early farming cultures of that region.[7]

The origin of the Indus Valley people is not clear. Because of their contact with cultures in

Afghanistan, Iran, Arabia, and south-central Asia, it is believed they may have originated from one or more of these areas. Some scholars claim that they were indigenous Dravidians.

3.6 Indus Priest/king

As a result of climate change and probably the arrival of Aryans from the north, these people eventually abandoned the Indus Valley and shifted to other parts of India.

There are no concrete records, but the world population in 5000 BCE is estimated to have been about five million.[8] On average, India's share of the world population has been about twenty percent. On this basis, the estimated population of the entire Indian subcontinent at that time, including the Indus Valley, was only about one million.

4000 BCE: Indo-Aryans

Located between the Caspian and the Aral Seas, the Amu Darya or Oxus River runs from the Pamir Mountains and generally forms the border between Tajikistan, Afghanistan, Uzbekistan, and Turkmenistan. The BMAC (Bactria-Margiana Archaeological Complex) located in a site called Gonur represents a Bronze Age civilization, known as the Oxus Civilization, of around 4000 BCE. These sites were discovered and named by the Soviet archaeologist Viktor Sarianidi.

Driven by what appears to be ecological changes, the people of this civilization moved southwest to Iran and southeast to India through the Hindu Kush mountain range. They were called Aryans ("noble" or "civilized" ones in Sanskrit), and those who came into India became known as Indo-Aryans.

Although there are different opinions about the origin of these people, the BMAC is considered a major settlement for their ancestors. Among his findings, Sarianidi discovered evidence of sacred altars; traces of ingredients such as poppy seeds, cannabis, and ephedra, used for a drink called *soma*; horse sacrifices; four-wheeled chariots; and other connections with the Aryan teachings.[9]

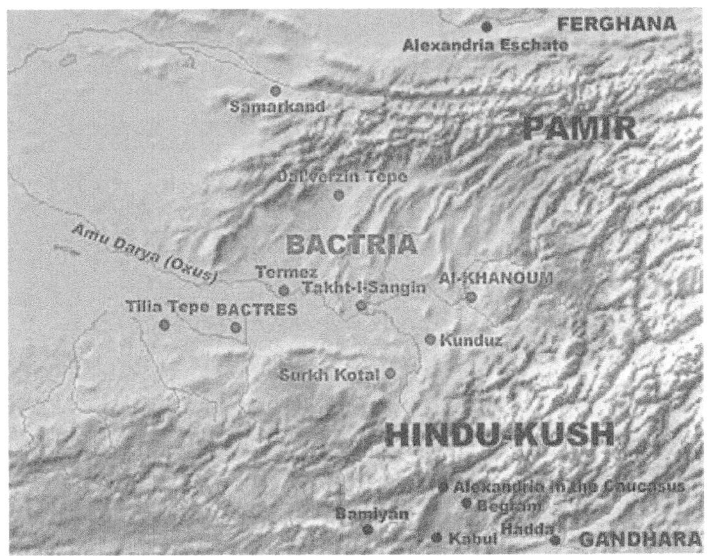

3.7 Bactria-Margiana

BMAC materials have been found in the Indus Valley sites as well. Academics like Asko Parpola, an Indologist at the University of Helsinki in Finland, and J. P. Mallory, an archaeologist from Queens University in Ireland and editor of the

Journal of Indo-European Studies, have also associated the Aryans with the BMAC.[10] As we will see in a later section, the genes of many people in India can be traced back to the BMAC area and Central Asia as well.

It appears that Aryans came to India in waves and brought with them what are known as Indo-Aryan or Indo-European languages. Migrations started around 1500 BCE when the Indus Valley civilization began to decline.

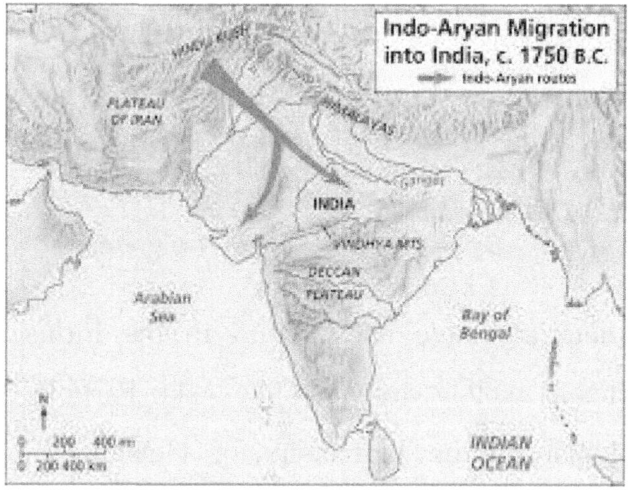

3.8 Aryan Movements

The nomadic Aryans were a cattle-breeding society, and they settled in northwest India as agriculturists. They conflicted with the indigenous people and pushed them out to other parts of India. Somewhere along the line, the Aryans domesticated the elephant, which was used in battles with Alexander the Great.

Aryans integrated the Indus culture into their own to form what came to be known as the Vedic culture. This civilization is associated with four texts known as the Vedas ("knowledge" or "wisdom"), and these became the sacred texts of Hinduism, the third-largest religion in the world. The first text, the Rig Veda, contains 1,028 verses; the other three are the Sama Veda, the Yajur Veda, and the Atharva Veda. The Vedas contain hymns (verses in praise of gods), philosophy, and other guidance. They represent the oldest teachings of India, though the transmission of these teachings was mainly oral until around 500 CE when they were written down.

The caste system in India refers to a stratified social hierarchy. It is generally attributed to the Aryans. The Rig Veda mentions four castes: Brahman, Rajanya, Vaisya, and Sudra.

Based on an individual's profession and duties, this type of social division became the Hindu *varna* system. The Brahman were the priests and teachers, the Rajanya (later known as the Kshatriya) were the ruling class and warriors, the Vaisya represented the merchants and agriculturists, and the Sudra were the general working class, including servants. Certain groups, later known as Dalits or the "untouchables," were excluded from the varna system.

As explained earlier, there is controversy about the origin of the Aryans. Some Indian scientists and academics claim that speakers of the Indo-Aryan languages are indigenous to the Indian subcontinent and that Indo-European languages originated in India.

550 BCE: The Persians

The First Persian Empire, also known as the Achaemenid Empire, was founded by Cyrus the Great (559-530 BCE). This empire stretched from Thrace and Macedon on the northeastern border of Greece to the Indus Valley.

After Cyrus, the kingdom was ruled by Darius I (521-486 BCE). The Persians ruled Taxila, now in Pakistan, in this period.

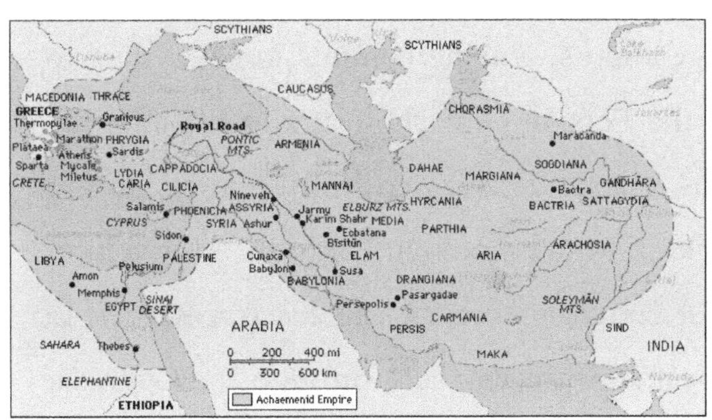

3.9 The Persian Empire.

326 BCE: Alexander the Great

At the age of thirty, Alexander the Great (356-323 BCE) began his invasion into India in 326 BCE. One year later, he fought an epic battle against the Indian king Porus of the Hindu Paurava kingdom on the banks of the Jhelum River in Punjab, now in Pakistan. After his victory, he made an alliance with Porus and appointed him a Macedonian satrap (local ruler).

Alexander appointed some Greek forces in Taxila and conquered areas around the Indus River down to the Arabian Sea. He sent a large contingent of his army to Carmania (modern southern Iran) with his general, Craterus, and he commissioned a fleet to explore the Persian Gulf shore under his admiral, Nearchus. Alexander was critically injured during his attack on Multan, now in Pakistan. After a brief period of convalescence, he led his forces back to Persia by the southern route through the Gedrosia (modern Makran in southern Pakistan).

After his death in 323 BCE, a series of fierce struggles among his followers destroyed his empire, and the territories were divided among his generals.

One of the commanders, Seleucus, established himself in Babylon. He expanded his territory as far as the western portions of India.

322–185 BCE: Mauryan Empire

Chandragupta Maurya (r. 322-298 BCE), a contemporary of Alexander the Great and one of the greatest leaders in Indian history, was the first emperor to unify India into one state. He became well known for conquering Alexander's eastern satrapies (areas controlled by a local ruler) and for defeating Seleucus in battle. Chandragupta and Seleucus reached an agreement about the border, formalized an alliance, and established a policy of friendship.

Chandragupta ended up marrying Seleucus's daughter, Helen, bringing Greek genes into his offspring. Thus, Chandragupta's son, Bindusara (r. 298-272 BCE), and grandson, Ashoka (r. 268-232 BCE), another great emperor in the history of India, were partly Greek.

Seleucus sent Megasthenes, a historian and diplomat, as his ambassador to the court of Chandragupta. Megasthenes wrote a detailed account of India, the *Indica*, in four volumes, most of which are lost. Among many things, he mentioned there were seven castes in Indian society during this time (compared to four in the Rig Veda during the Aryan period).

Under Chandragupta's rule, almost all parts of India became united under a single government, thus establishing the Mauryan Empire. At that time, Indian borders touched Persia and Central Asia. He conquered Gandhara and several areas of the northwest parts of India. After many conquests, Chandragupta resigned, became a Jain monk, and ended his life by ritually fasting to death.

His son, Bindusara, assumed the throne and ruled India for many years. Bindusara's son, Ashoka, conquered more territories. After seeing the enormous death and destruction he had caused in the Kalinga War, he stopped the policy of conquering new areas. He became a Buddhist and started to follow the path of *ahimsa* (not to injure). He sent persons to several parts of India, China, and Sri Lanka to preach Buddhism.

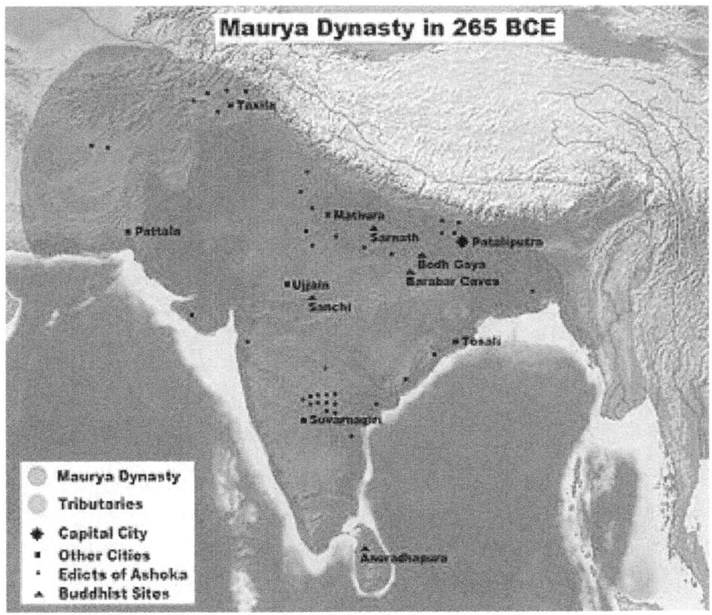

3.10 The Mauryan Empire

Ashoka ruled most of India as it stands today. He built a number of stupas and pillars across the country with inscriptions of his understanding of Buddhist doctrines.

His lion pillar is the emblem of India today. Brihadratha (r. 187-185 BCE) was the last ruler of the Mauryan Empire.

Kautalya, also known as Chanakya (Chanakyapuri, the diplomatic enclave of New Delhi, is named after him), guided Chandragupta Maurya and his sons in founding and expanding the great Mauryan Empire. He composed the *Arthashastra*, a treatise on statecraft, economic policy, and military strategy. The book includes the memorable saying, "My enemy's enemy is my friend."

3.11 Ashoka's Lion Pillar

This work was written in Taxila several hundred years before Niccolò Machiavelli composed a similar treatise, *The Prince*, in Italy.

200 BCE TO 10 CE: GREEKS IN INDIA

After the Mauryan Dynasty, Indo-Greeks, who were remnants of Alexander the Great's forces, returned to power in various parts of northwestern India. They ruled from about 200 BCE to 10 CE and were eventually conquered by the Indo-Scythians and Kushans. A part of the following time line is based on an extensive study of excavated coins from this period by Sri Lankan historian and numismatist Osmund Bopearachchi.[11]

Demetrius I (r. 200–190 BCE) was the first ruler and founder of the Indo-Greek kingdom.

Menander I (r. 155–130 BCE) ruled over the eastern divided Greek empire of Bactria along with the northwest Frontier Province and Punjab in Pakistan and Punjab, Haryana, and parts of Himachal Pradesh and the Jammu region in present-day India. His capital is supposed to have been modern Sialkot in Pakistan.

Based on one of his coins, Thraso (possibly ruled around 130 BCE) was an Indo-Greek king in central and western Punjab. Philoxenus Anicetus (r. 125–110 BCE) was an Indo-Greek king who ruled in the region spanning the Paropamisadae (the ancient Greek name for a region of the Hindu Kush in eastern Afghanistan) to Punjab.

Agathokleia Theotropos (r. 110–100 BCE) was an Indo-Greek queen who ruled in parts of northern India as regent for her son, Strato I. Although not fully corroborated, after losing some territory, Strato I (r. 110–85 BCE) is believed to have ruled over Gandhara and western Punjab.

Artemidoros Aniketos (possibly ruled around 100 to 80 BCE) was a king who ruled the areas of Gandhara and Pushkalavati in modern northern Pakistan and

3.12 Menander silver coin

Afghanistan.

Epander (r. 95–90 BCE) was an Indo-Greek king whose coins seem to indicate that he ruled the area of Punjab.

Heliocles II (r. 95–80 BCE) was another Indo-Greek king who ruled over parts of the northwest.

Archebios (r. 90–70 BCE) ruled the area of Taxila. Telephos Euergetes (r. 75–70 BCE) was a late Indo-Greek king in Gandhara who appears to have been a brief successor of Maues.

Strato II and III (r. 25 BCE to 10 CE) ruled in eastern Punjab and retained Sialkot as the capital.

120 BCE: Yuezhi Incursions

The first significant appearance of the Xiongnu, fierce nomadic people who were likely the ancestors of the Huns, was in central China around 300 BCE. The Great Wall of China, which is about thirteen thousand miles long, was built in part to protect the Chinese Empire against intrusions from such nomadic groups. The Chinese were successful and repelled an invasion of the Xiongnu, pushing them toward the west.

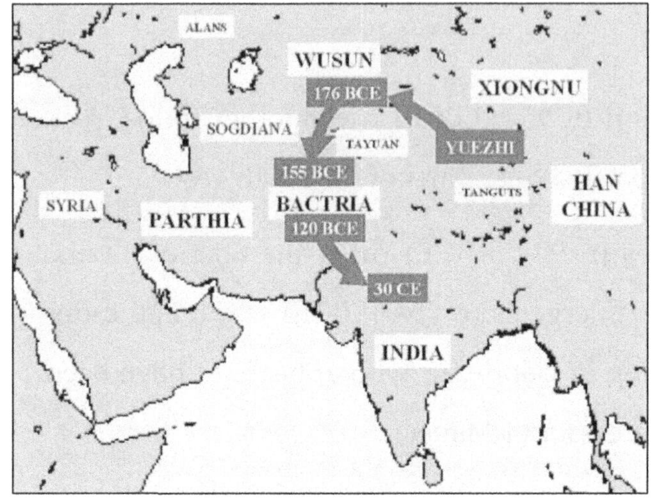

3.13 The Yuezhi migrations

The Xiongnu turned their attention toward the Yuezhi, an ancient people who originally settled in what is today Xinjiang and western Gansu in China. The Yuezhi were driven west by the Xiongnu to the borderlands of what is now Afghanistan, Pakistan, Tajikistan, and Uzbekistan, where they established an independent empire in the region of Bactria. In Bactria, they conquered the Scythians and the local

Indo-Greek kingdoms, the last of Alexander the Great's forces that had failed to take India.

3.14 The Great Wall of China
(Copyright © David G. Mahal)

Early in the second century, the Yuezhi began to appear in the Oxus Valley (modern Amu Darya). They defeated the Scythians who occupied the area and pushed them south. Of the five Yuezhi chieftains, one branch founded the Kushan Empire, which extended its power south and east into India and north into Central Asia.

110 BCE TO 395 CE: INDO-SCYTHIANS

Scythians (also called Sakas) were nomadic people who migrated from Central Asia to southern Russia in the eighth and seventh centuries BCE. They developed a class of wealthy aristocrats, known as Royal Scyths, who ruled southern Russian and Crimean territories. The Persian king Darius I attacked these territories in about 513 BCE and was unsuccessful. The community was destroyed in the second century BCE, and it dispersed in different directions.

The term *Indo-Scythian* is used to refer to Scythians who migrated into parts of Central Asia and South Asia from the middle of the second century BCE. The initial migration of the Scythians led them to Kashmir. More Scythians came to India, passing through Bactria, Sogdiana, Kashmir, and Afghanistan.

After entering the Indian subcontinent through Afghanistan, the first Indo-Scythian kingdom occupied the southern areas from Sindh in Pakistan to Gujarat in India from around 110–80 BCE. These people gradually moved north into Indo-Greek territory, defeated the Indo-Greek rulers of northwest India, and established an Indo-Scythian kingdom in India.[12]

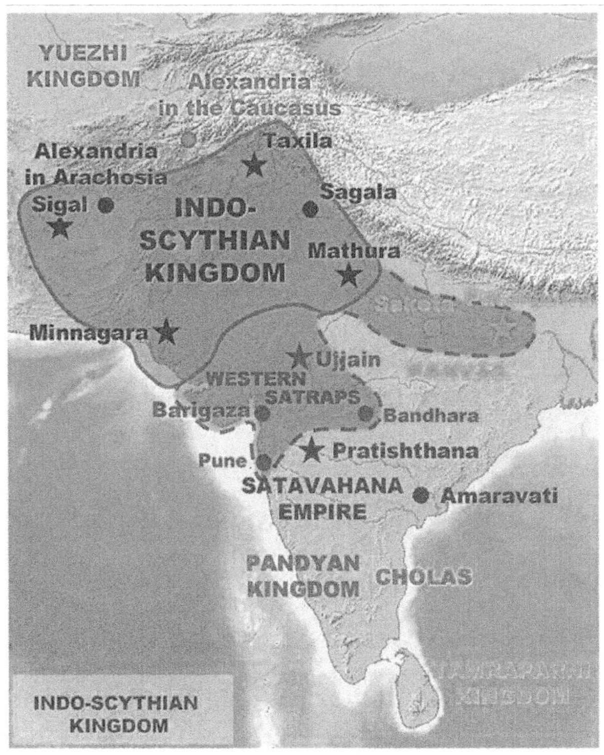

3.15 Indo-Scythian Kingdom

Based in Gandhara, the first Indo-Scythian king was Maues (r. 85–60 BCE). Also known as Moga, he ruled over most of northwestern India. After the death of Azes, the last king, Indo-Scythian rule declined during the latter part of the first century BCE. A number of minor leaders continued in local strongholds. The Indo-Scythian kingdom ended in 395 CE when Chandragupta II killed the last ruler.

30–335 CE: The Kushan Empire

The Kushan Empire was formed in the early first century CE under Kujula Kadphises in the territories around the Oxus River (Amu Darya) and later near Kabul, Afghanistan. The Kushans spread from the Kabul River valley to defeat Central Asian tribes that had conquered parts of the north-central Iranian Plateau, once ruled by the Parthians. They reached their peak under the Buddhist emperor Kanishka (who was of Yuezhi ethnicity), whose realm stretched from Turfan in the Tarim Basin to Pataliputra (Patna) in India.

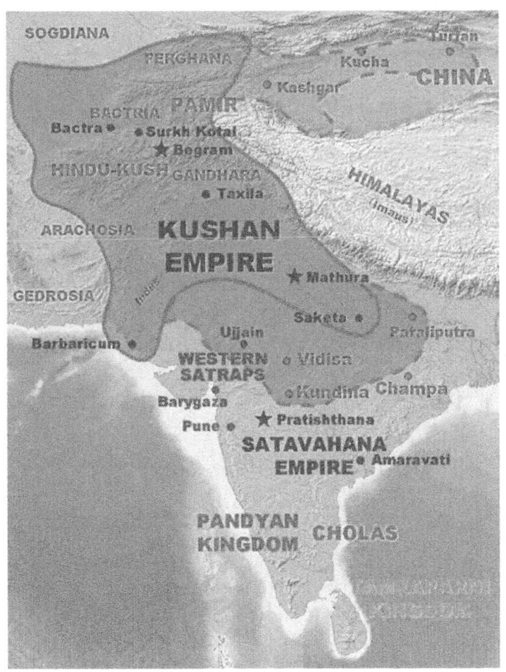

3.16 The Kushan Empire

Predominantly Zoroastrian, the Kushans incorporated Buddhist and Hellenistic beliefs into their religious practices. Kushan coins depict deities ranging from Helios and Heracles to the Buddha, Ahura Mazda, Mithra, and Atar, the Zoroastrian fire god. They used the Greek alphabet and altered it to suit spoken Kushan. The last of the Kushans were overwhelmed by the White Huns.

127–151 CE: Kanishka the Great

Under Kanishka, the Kushan Empire expanded into northern India. Kanishka ruled from Peshawar, now in Pakistan, and the major Silk Road (trade routes in Asia) cities of Kashgar, Yarkand, and Khotan in what is now Xinjiang or east Turkestan. Kanishka was a devout Buddhist and has been compared to the Mauryan emperor Ashoka the Great. Evidence suggests that he worshipped the Persian deity Mithra. After 225 CE, the Kushan Empire crumbled into a western half that was conquered by the Sassanid Empire of Persia and an eastern half with its capital in the Punjab. The eastern Kushan Empire fell, likely between 335 and 350 CE, to the Gupta king Samudragupta.

500 CE: Invasion of the Huns

The Huns were descendants of the Xiongnu, a group of fierce, warlike, nomadic herders from the steppes of north-central Asia, north of China

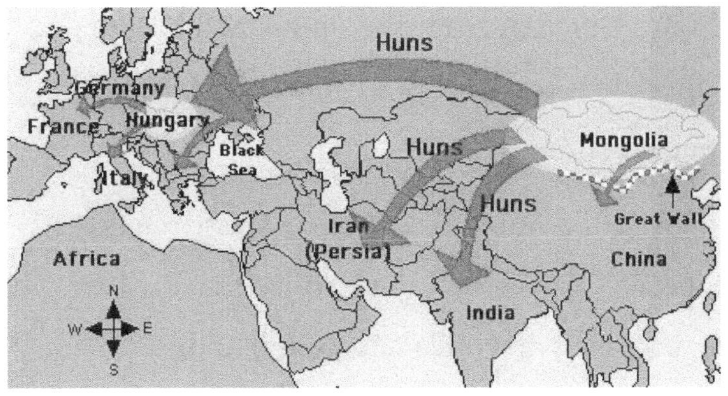

3.17 Invasions of the Huns

(Mongolia). They pushed the Yuezhi out of the area, and during their migrations, they split into two groups. One group went as far as Scythia, modern-day southern Russia and Kazakhstan, where they conquered a number of local tribes.

Attila the Hun (406–453 CE) and his warriors rose from the plains of Scythia and spread terror across Europe. The European Huns settled in what is now Hungary.

Another group, later called the White Huns (in Greek, Hephthalites; in Sanskrit, Sveta Huna), moved into Afghanistan and made Bamiyan their capital city. Different from the Huns under Attila, the White Huns were believed to have white skin and elongated heads.

During the fifth century, the Gupta Dynasty reigned in the Ganges basin of India, while the Kushan Empire occupied the area along the Indus. The Huns eventually conquered the Kushans. After the last of the Gupta rulers, Skandagupta, died in 467 CE, they entered India and destroyed many cities and towns along the Ganges.

They persecuted Buddhists and burned their monasteries. Their conquest was accomplished with extreme ferocity, and the Gupta regime was destroyed.

Based on their coins and inscriptions, Toramana and his son Mihirakula (Mehrgul) were the most famous Hun kings who ruled in northern India. Some historians believe that the Huns intermarried with the indigenous people and were absorbed into the Indian population.[13]

1162–1227 CE: GENGHIS KHAN

Genghis Khan, the fearsome Mongolian warrior of the thirteenth century, may have done more than rule the largest empire in the world. According to a recently published genetic study, he may have helped increase the population as well.

3.18 Genghis Khan

An international group of geneticists found that nearly 8 percent of the men living in the region of the former Mongol Empire carry genes that are nearly identical. That translates to 0.5 percent of the male population in the world, or roughly sixteen million descendants living today.[14]

In the early sixteenth century, descendants of Genghis Khan swept across the Khyber Pass and established the Mughal Dynasty, which lasted for three hundred years.

1527–1857 CE: Mughal Empire

The Mughal emperors were Central-Asian Turks from Uzbekistan who claimed to be descended from both Timur and Genghis Khan. Timur's great-great-grandson, Babur, founded the Islamic Empire and ruled over most of Afghanistan and North India.

Babur's descendants (Humayun, Akbar, Jahangir, Shah Jahan, and Aurangzeb) expanded the Mughal Empire to most of the Indian subcontinent.

The greatest part of the Mughal expansion was accomplished during the reign of Akbar the Great (1556–1605), a freethinking Muslim, under whose rule the empire tripled in size and wealth. Akbar abolished the sectarian tax on non-Muslims, employed locals in his administration, and, to bring about religious unity, tried to create a new religion based on Islam, Hinduism, Zoroastrianism, and Christianity.

Padmini, a Hindu Rajput princess, became one of his many wives.

3.19 Taj Mahal, Agra

Sher Shah Suri (1486-1545), a Pashtun Afghan known as "the Lion King" (for reportedly killing a lion with his bare hands), rebelled against the Mughal rule and overthrew Babur's son, Humayun, in 1540. His short-lived sultanate in Delhi fell to Humayun again in 1555, and the Mughal Empire continued.

Shah Jahan, the fifth emperor, erected historical monuments in India, including the Taj Mahal at

Agra, the Red Fort, and Jama Masjid at Delhi. The Taj Mahal was built as a monument to his wife, Mumtaz Mahal, who bore fourteen children and died during childbirth. Named a UNESCO World Heritage Site in 1983, the Taj Mahal is one of the finest examples of Mughal architecture.

The Mughal Empire became well known in faraway lands. In Europe, the famous Italian composer and priest Antonio Vivaldi (1678–1741) composed and dedicated two concertos for strings, *Concerto Grosso Mogul* and *Il Gran Mogul,* to the Mughal Empire. It is unknown if these concertos, composed for Western instruments, were ever played for the Mughal emperors in India. After Aurangzeb, the empire went into rapid decline.

India: A Genetic Forest

There were other regimes after the Moghuls. The British came to India as traders and set up the British East India Company. As the Moghul Empire deteriorated, the British took advantage of local conflicts and became conquerors of the entire country. In addition to the British, there were other arrivals, such as the Portuguese, the Dutch, and the French. During World War II, even the Japanese occupied the Andaman and Nicobar Islands for about three years. The British ruled India as a colony for more than three hundred years and left in 1947 after carving East Pakistan (now Bangladesh) and West Pakistan (now Pakistan) from Indian territory.

The following is only a partial list of the ethnic types that have arrived in India over the years.

- Afghans
- Africans
- Arabs
- Armenians
- Aryans
- British
- Chinese
- Dutch
- French
- Greeks
- Huns
- Iranians
- Japanese
- Jews
- Kushans
- Mongols
- Parsees
- Persians
- Portuguese
- Scythians
- Syrians
- Tajiks
- Turks
- Uzbeks

During the convergence of ethnic groups, many migrants and invaders intermarried and mixed with the local people. This resulted in a highly mixed pool of foreign genes in India. Dr. B. S. Ahloowalia, author of *Invasion of the Genes*, explains it this way:

> No other region ever experienced such traumatic changes and with such frequency as North India. The scale and frequency of the invasions was so huge and left such an immense impact on the introduction and spread of new genes, that the invasions can be rightly called gene invasions.[15]

With a multitude of different ethnic communities with their own languages and dialects, India has been aptly described as an "ethnological museum."

Chapter 4
Counting Ancestors

> It is likely that 80 percent of all marriages in history have been between second cousins or closer.
> —Robin Fox

Most of us know or remember our grandparents, and we may have heard the names of our great-grandparents. We may know where these relatives lived and what they did for a living. Because of better medical care, members of several generations may be living at the same time, but typically our knowledge about our family trees goes back only a few generations. Most of us know little or nothing about our earlier relatives, but the number of these earlier relatives is large, and the details may astound you. Population grows exponentially fast. If a woman's childbearing years are from sixteen to forty and she gives birth every two years, she can have twelve children. On average, six of these children will be girls, and they will grow up to be mothers. With each mother producing six more mothers, eight people can rapidly multiply into several million in a few hundred years. Assuming twenty-five years per generation, we find the following:

- One generation, or twenty-five years ago, you had two parents.
- Two generations, or fifty years ago, you had four grandparents.
- Three generations, or seventy-five years ago, you had eight great-grandparents.

Every generation has twice as many ancestors as the generation before. As shown in the family tree in chart 4.1 (which starts with the year 2000 for convenience), if you go back nine generations, or about two hundred years, more than five hundred people were responsible for your existence. Go back twenty generations, or about five hundred years, and there were more than a million ancestors. If you go back thirty generations, you'll find that you had well over one billion ancestors, nearly the current population of all India. Go back thirty-three generations, and the number of ancestors exceeds eight billion, more than the current population of the world. If you keep going back, eventually the answer exceeds the number of people who have ever lived on this planet. Obviously, this mathematical conclusion is incorrect. So what is going on?

The explanation is that many slots on a family tree are filled by the same people. A large number of ancestors are counted repeatedly, and there is a lot of duplication in the numbers. The actual number of ancestors in a family tree is far less than the mathematical answer, and you have "many" but not billions of distinct ancestors.

This phenomenon gets more pronounced the further back one goes, so a smaller proportion of one's family tree consists of "distinct" people with each generation. This type of reduction in the number of ancestors has a simple explanation.

Pedigree Collapse

Normally, a person has eight great-grandparents. However, someone who marries his or her first cousin has only six individuals as great-grandparents, because two of them are duplicates. This type of reduction in the number of ancestors in a family tree is known as "pedigree collapse."

The primary reason for this phenomenon is that for much of history, many people stayed in the same place their entire lives. In historical communities that had no access to efficient transportation, sexual relationships and marriages most frequently took place between people living near each other, and spouses were often drawn from a pool of close relatives, sometimes from within the family.

English genealogist, physicist, and computer programmer Brian Pears says, "If every single marriage was between second cousins, then 30 generations ago [residents of Britain] would all have needed exactly 4,356,616 ancestors."[1] The mass movement of humans in the last few centuries has changed this phenomenon, and people tend to have far more diverse family trees than in the past. According to a recent survey, all Europeans living today are related to the same set of ancestors who lived one thousand years ago.[2]

Pedigree collapse occurs whenever one ancestor reproduces with someone to whom he or she is related. The numbers in chart 4.1 contain many ancestors who are duplicates and appear more than once. Looking back in one's family history, it is challenging to determine how many ancestors were real and how many were duplicates. The best we can do is estimate.

The Revised Family Tree

If we assume that 30 percent of the ancestors in each generation in the family tree shown in chart 4.1 are duplicates, we can make a simple mathematical adjustment. The revised chart 4.2 on the following page shows that the number of ancestors a thousand years ago even after a 30 percent reduction in each generation is well over one million. Of course, this is not a precise result. Suffice it to say that the number of our ancestors is very large.

According to the *Atlas of World Population History*, the estimated population of the Indian subcontinent in CE 1000 was about 80 million. As described earlier, these people came from many different parts of the globe, intermingled, and multiplied. In a little over one thousand years this group mushroomed into a population of over one billion people. Our family trees emerge from the depths of this pool of humanity.

Generations	Year	Ancestors
1	2000	2
2	1975	4
3	1950	8
4	1925	16
5	1900	32
6	1875	64
7	1850	128
8	1825	256
9	1800	512
10	1775	1,024
11	1750	2,048
12	1725	4,096
13	1700	8,192
14	1675	16,384
15	1650	32,768
16	1625	65,536
17	1600	131,072
18	1575	262,144
19	1550	524,288
20	1525	1,048,576
21	1500	2,097,152
22	1475	4,194,304
23	1450	8,388,608
24	1425	16,777,216
25	1400	33,554,432
26	1375	67,108,864
27	1350	134,217,728
28	1325	268,435,456
29	1300	536,870,912
30	1275	1,073,741,824
31	1250	2,147,483,648
32	1225	4,294,967,296
33	1200	8,589,934,592
34	1175	17,179,869,184
35	1150	34,359,738,368
36	1125	68,719,476,736
37	1100	137,438,953,472
38	1075	274,877,906,944
39	1050	549,755,813,888
40	1025	1,099,511,627,776
41	1000	2,199,023,255,552

4.1 Family Tree

Generations	Year	Ancestors
1	2000	2
2	1975	3
3	1950	4
4	1925	5
5	1900	8
6	1875	11
7	1850	15
8	1825	21
9	1800	30
10	1775	41
11	1750	58
12	1725	81
13	1700	113
14	1675	159
15	1650	222
16	1625	311
17	1600	436
18	1575	610
19	1550	854
20	1525	1,195
21	1500	1,673
22	1475	2,343
23	1450	3,280
24	1425	4,592
25	1400	6,428
26	1375	9,000
27	1350	12,600
28	1325	17,640
29	1300	24,695
30	1275	34,573
31	1250	48,403
32	1225	67,764
33	1200	94,870
34	1175	132,817
35	1150	185,944
36	1125	260,322
37	1100	364,451
38	1075	510,232
39	1050	714,324
40	1025	1,000,054
41	1000	1,400,075

4.2 Family Tree after 30% Reduction

PART TWO
DNA ROOTS

This part covers the science of genes and genealogy. It describes the Human Genome Project, which surveyed the genetic design of the human being. There are explanations about what genes are and how DNA analysis is used to more accurately trace ancestry. This part also includes a research study of the DNA results of key ethnic communities from the Indian subcontinent. The results of the study applicable to the Jat population are explained.

CHAPTER 5
GENES AND GENEALOGY

> Without a doubt, this is the most important, most wondrous map ever produced by humankind.
> —Bill Clinton

In 1990, four-year-old Ashanti DeSilva of Indian heritage became the first person to receive gene therapy at the University of Southern California in Los Angeles. DeSilva suffered from a rare inherited immune disorder known as adenosine deaminase (ADA) deficiency, which severely compromised her immune system. Without the enzyme that would protect her from bacteria and viruses, she was likely to die prematurely.

She was injected with her own white blood cells that had been modified with a healthy version of her defective genes. Her treatment was a success, but gene therapy has had mixed results. In 1999, Jesse Gelsinger, an eighteen-year-old from Arizona, became the first patient to die from gene therapy rather than the disease he was suffering from.[1] There have been other cases where gene therapy did not work properly. Not all endeavors succeed immediately.

Scientists are working to translate the promise of gene therapy into treatments for a variety of medical conditions. For instance, medical practitioners are aware that a drug at the recommended standard dose does not work in the same manner for everyone. Researchers at the Mayo Clinic are studying how a patient's genes influence his or her response to medicines. The goal is to deliver the right drug at the right dose—a 'customized' drug, so to speak—and provide the best medical treatment based on a patient's specific genes.[2] This knowledge about our genes is having profound impacts in the fields of medicine, biotechnology, the life sciences, forensics, and ancestry. It has become possible to study genes in depth only recently; our grandparents could not have dreamed of such advances.

The Human Genome Project

Launched in 1990, the Human Genome Project (HGP) was a three-billion-dollar joint project between the US Department of Energy and the National Institutes of Health. The goal was to uncover the complete sequence of human DNA (genes are part of DNA). It became a massive international effort to determine the identity and location of the nearly three billion molecules that make up human DNA. In 1998, Celera Genomics, a private, venture-capital-funded company founded by Craig Venter, launched an effort to achieve the same goal. Because of such international efforts, the project was completed ahead of schedule.

On June 26, 2000, President Bill Clinton held a ceremony in the White House to celebrate the completion of the survey of the entire human genome. Tony Blair, the prime minister of England, joined him in this announcement via satellite. The results of the survey allowed researchers all over the world to begin to understand the internal blueprint of human beings. As our understanding of genetics, human diseases, and the aging process expands, it may be possible for people to regularly live one hundred years or more by the end of this century. This new science has also allowed us to explore our ancestry by analyzing our genes.

DNA and Ancestry

The frozen, 5,300-year-old body of *Ötzi the Iceman* was found in the Italian Alps in 1991. It is reported that there are at least nineteen genetic relatives of Ötzi living in the Tyrol region of Austria today. Researchers found nineteen genetic matches by analyzing DNA records of 3,700 Austrian blood donors. Scientists expect to find more living relatives of Ötzi in the nearby Swiss and Italian

Alps.[3] These results were accomplished through recent advances in DNA testing.

As discussed earlier, it is relatively simple to identify ancestors going back a few hundred years. Beyond that, the task is complicated, because for most of us, there is no documentation. Luckily, there are new methods for tracing our ancestry. Because we inherit our DNA from our parents, we can track the genes in our DNA back thousands of years and determine where our ancestors came from. Genetic tests allow us to trace the path of ancestors and find out who they were, where they lived, and how they dispersed throughout the world. We can learn how we came to be where we are today.

The science of genetic or DNA testing has evolved rapidly in recent years. These days, laboratories in many parts of the world routinely perform such tests. To collect DNA, all that is usually needed is a sample from the mouth—a painless swab of the inside of the cheek or a small amount of saliva. The laboratories conduct the test and provide a written report. Some laboratories perform the test anonymously and post the results, which can be accessed only with a secret code, on their website.

It is unnecessary for the average person to become an expert in the science of DNA testing, but it is useful to know the basic terminology and understand how the tests are performed and interpreted. Let us briefly review how DNA can be used to trace ancestry. It will provide awesome insights into our bodies.

THE HUMAN CELL

All living beings are made of cells, which are the building blocks of life and are invisible to our eyes. The human body contains fifty to one hundred trillion microscopic cells, which are the smallest units of living matter. There are many different types of cells—blood, muscle, brain, hair, skin, fat, and many others. Each type of cell has its own purpose. For example, the cells in our eyes control vision and heart muscle cells control how the heart functions. Some cells, such as those in the hair and skin, replicate frequently. Others, such as those in the central nervous system (the brain), rarely reproduce.

All cells have a similar structure. An outer membrane contains a nucleus that controls the cell, and the nucleus has its own membrane. The instructions that tell the cell what to do reside in the nucleus. These instructions are in the form of long, threadlike chemical molecules called chromosomes. Ordinarily, the chromosomes are loosely packed and not visible even under a microscope. They become visible only when the cell divides and replicates.

There are two types of sex chromosomes: X and Y. The nucleus of the cell for a female contains only X chromosomes, and the nucleus of the cell for a male contains both X and Y chromosomes.

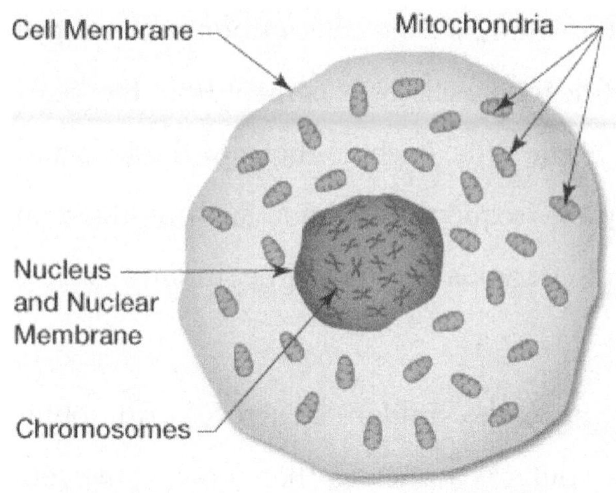

5.1 Human cell (courtesy of FamilyTreeDNA.com).

Each human cell contains forty-six chromosomes that are intertwined in twenty-three pairs. One member of each chromosome pair is inherited from the father, and one is inherited from the mother. Of the twenty-three chromosome pairs, twenty-two pairs look the same in both males and females, and these are called autosomes. The twenty-third pair is different—it contains the sex chromosomes and differentiates males from females.

If the X chromosome is inherited from the father with another X coming from the mother, the child is a female with two copies of the X chromosome (XX). If the Y chromosome is inherited from the father with the X coming from the mother, the child is a male with one X and one Y chromosome (XY). This is why it is said that the father determines the sex of a child.

DNA

DNA stands for deoxyribonucleic acid, and it carries all of our genetic information. The chromosomes are made of strands of DNA. All the cells in the body, except red blood cells, contain a copy of the DNA, and nearly every cell has the same DNA. For all humans, 99.9 percent of DNA is identical, but the remaining 0.1 percent represents about three million differences between any two people. Therefore, except for identical twins, each person's DNA is unique. We are all similar and yet different. A short segment of DNA can serve as a "fingerprint" that is unique to each person. This is how people are identified by using their DNA.

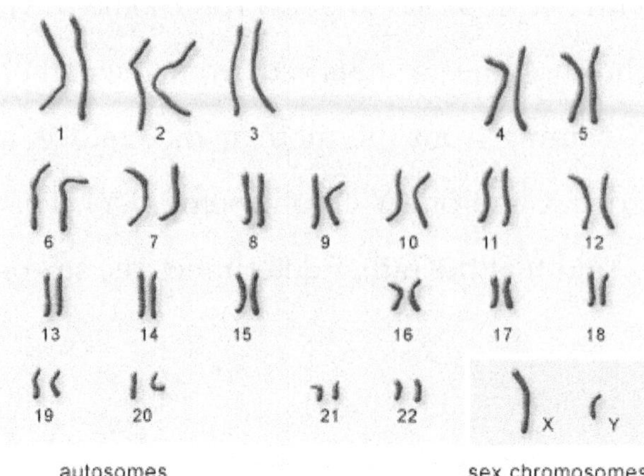

5.2 Autosomes and sex chromosomes
(courtesy of the US National Library of Medicine)

The thin DNA strands in one cell can stretch to more than six feet (two meters) in length, and all of the DNA in the human body weighs about one-quarter of an ounce (about seven and a half grams). If all the strands of DNA were placed end to end, it could theoretically stretch from the earth to the sun and back. The exact number of genes in the body is unknown, but the human genome contains the complete set of an estimated thirty thousand genes.

There are two types of DNA, nuclear and mitochondrial (see figure 5.1). DNA located in the nucleus of the cell is called nuclear DNA. A small amount of DNA is found outside the nucleus in an area known as a mitochondrion; it is called mitochondrial DNA.

All males have one Y-chromosome in each cell. The Y chromosome is passed down from father to son and remains virtually unchanged (there is mutation but the rate is low) from one generation to the next. The Y chromosome (known as Y-DNA) traces a paternal line. Both males and females inherit X chromosomes and mitochondria from their mothers. The X chromosome and mitochondria is passed down from mothers to their children—both male and female—but only their daughters pass it on to the next generation. The X chromosome (known as MT-DNA) traces a maternal line.

The DNA molecule is contained in two complementary chains that wrap around each other to resemble a twisted ladder or staircase known as the *double helix*. The sides of the staircase are made of sugar and phosphate molecules. The stairs are made of nitrogen-containing chemicals called bases or nucleotides. Four different bases are present: adenine (A), thymine (T), cytosine (C), and guanine (G). The particular order of these four bases, called the DNA sequence or blueprint, guides protein production and how the cell functions.

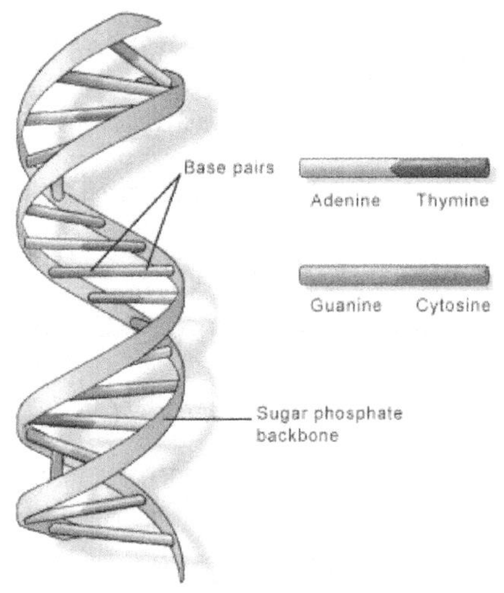

5.3. The double helix of DNA
(courtesy of the US National Library of Medicine).

The four bases, also known as base pairs, always pair up in a set manner; A pairs with T, while C pairs with G. The DNA sequence consists of a large number of A, C, G, and T nucleotides. There are about three billion base pairs in the human genome. A portion of the DNA strands on the double helix may look like this:

Strand 1: A-C-T-C-G-G-T-A-A

Strand 2: T-G-A-G-C-C-A-T-T

When a cell divides for reproduction, the helix unwinds, splits down the middle, and copies itself to a new cell.

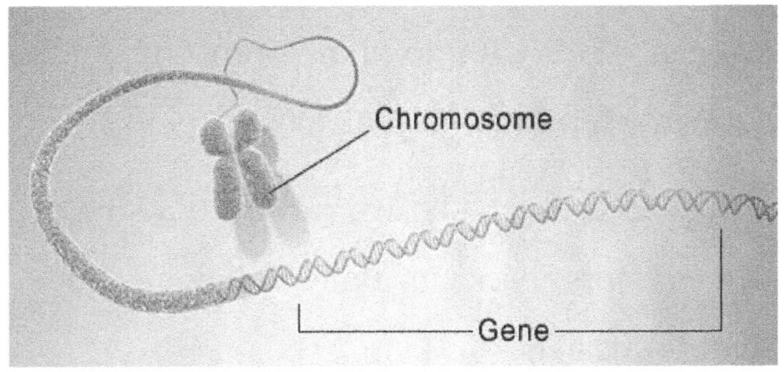

5.4 Genes on DNA Strand (courtesy of the US National Library of Medicine)

There is an ongoing daily molecular war in the nucleus of the human cell. DNA damage occurs at the rate of 20,000 lesions per cell per day.[4] This is caused by exposure to factors commonly found in food, water, air, and toxic materials, as well as by-products of one's own metabolism. Most people ordinarily sustain these attacks and remain healthy; when they cannot do so, they become sick.

GENES

The entire DNA strand does not contain genes. The genes are contained only on short sections of the DNA strands. Less than 2 percent of a person's total DNA represents genes, so there are long stretches of DNA between genes with no known function, and these are often referred to as "junk DNA."

Given any gene in the body, we can trace a single chain of ancestors back in time, following the lineage of this one gene.

Because a typical organism is built from tens of thousands of genes, there are many ways to trace ancestry using this mechanism. This is done by analyzing markers and mutations in the DNA sequence of a person.

MARKERS

A marker is a segment of the DNA that is associated with genetic characteristics. The markers are found at certain locations or *loci* (plural of *locus,* meaning place) on the chromosome where a base pattern is repeated a number of times. The terms *marker* and *locus* are often used interchangeably and can be confusing. For clarity, the marker is what is tested, and the locus is where the marker is located. Each marker on the Y chromosome is designated by a DYS number (D for DNA, Y for Y chromosome, S for segment) that is used to search for genetic matches. There is a known range of values for each marker.

The HUGO Gene Nomenclature Committee (HGNC) in Cambridge, England, is the worldwide authority that approves and assigns names and symbols for the human gene. The HGNC has also assigned DYS numbers to the Y-STRs used in human genetic testing. In the following example, the four-base pattern TCTA appears six times at marker DYS391:

TCTATCTATCTATCTATCTATCTA

The number of times a pattern is repeated is known as the number of repeats or the *allele* value for that marker. In this case, the allele value of marker DYS391 is six. Once markers are identified, they can be traced to their origin or the individual called the "most recent common ancestor" of a group of individuals.

Two kinds of markers are used in genetic testing: short tandem repeats (STRs) and single nucleotide polymorphisms (SNPs). STRs and SNPs hold different types of information and are used for different purposes:

- STRs found on the Y chromosome are called Y-STRs and are used exclusively for tracing male lines of heredity.
- SNPs or "snips" are found on the Y chromosome and in MT-DNA. They are used for tracing male and female lines of heredity.

MUTATIONS

Where DNA is normally passed unchanged from parent to offspring, occasionally a random, naturally occurring, and usually harmless change occurs. Known as a mutation, the most common change occurs in a single base on the DNA sequence. For example, the base may change from a C to a G.

There can be other changes, such as the loss or addition of one or more bases. Although a mutation can change the instructions in a gene, most mutations have little or no impact.

Mutations can occur during a person's lifetime spontaneously or as the result of external factors, such as radiation or exposure to certain viruses. Mutations occur at a low rate in every generation with about fifty changes in the billions of nucleotides in the human genome.[5] That amounts to about once every five hundred generations per marker.

The mutations serve as beacons. They can be mapped, because they are passed down through generations for thousands of years. When geneticists identify a mutation, they try to figure out when it first occurred and in which geographic region of the world.

A mutation is usually the beginning of a new lineage on a family tree and can trace ancestors to a specific time and place in history.

By comparing the mutations in different people, geneticists can determine how closely they are related. By calculating the mutation rate, they can also determine how long ago and where people split from their ancient clans.

HAPLOTYPE

A haplotype is the set of results for tested markers. DNA testing companies use different markers for producing their results and present them differently. The number of markers examined varies from one testing company to another, but most tests use from nine to forty markers.

In a nine-marker test, the probability that two people selected randomly will match each other on all nine markers is less than two in one thousand.[6] The Genographic Project at the National Geographic Society uses the following twelve markers:

- DYS19
- DYS385a
- DYS385b
- DYS388
- DYS389-1
- DYS389-2
- DYS390
- DYS391
- DYS392
- DYS393
- DYS426
- DYS439

The common haplotype model used in Europe is called the Atlantic Modal Haplotype (AMH), and it uses the following six markers:

- DYS19

- DYS388
- DYS390
- DYS391
- DYS392
- DYS393

As an example, the typical results of a twelve-marker test for individual "A" may be presented as follows (the allele values appear under the DYS numbers).

Marker#	1	2	3	4	5	6	7	8	9	10	11	12
DYS #	19	389I	389II	390	391	392	393	385a	385b	426	439	388
A	14	12	29	22	10	11	12	15	18	10	13	14

To determine a genetic connection between individuals, the alleles are compared for each marker. The more alleles that match, the more likely it is that the individuals are related or have a common ancestor. Here is a comparison of the test results for four individuals labeled A, B, C, and D.

Marker#	1	2	3	4	5	6	7	8	9	10	11	12
DYS #	19	389I	389II	390	391	392	393	385a	385b	426	439	388
A	15	13	29	22	11	14	12	10	16	10	12	16
B	16	13	29	24	11	14	13	11	14	11	10	14
C	16	13	29	25	10	14	13	11	14	11	10	14
D	14	13	29	22	11	11	12	15	18	10	13	14

The results show that B and C have matching alleles for all markers with only small differences for the values in DYS390 and DYS391. In terms of their ancient DNA, B and C are more closely related compared to A and B and have a common ancestor in the past.

Haplogroup

Let us picture the entire human population as a large tree. A haplogroup is a branch of this tree, and a haplotype is a leaf on that branch. The haplogroup designates a cluster of people who have inherited common genetic markers from the same ancestor going back several thousand years. These designations allow genealogists to gain insights about direct paternal or maternal ancestors. The haplogroup is of primary interest to us in exploring our deep ancestry.

All humans belong to haplogroups, which are designated according to their Y-DNA and MT-DNA. The haplogroup for any person is determined with data from a haplotype by using a computational model or software.

The haplogroups contain many branches called subhaplogroups or subclades. The top-level haplogroups are expressed in letters (A, B, C, and so on). Their subhaplogroups or subclades are expressed in letters and numbers (G2, R1b1, E3b1b, and so on).

The Phylogenetic Tree

Phylogeography is the science of determining the place of origin and spread of genetic lineages. It involves the study of processes that may be responsible for the geographic distribution of human beings. It uses markers to assign people who share a set of genetic markers and therefore share an ancestor to their respective haplogroup.

The International Society of Genetic Geology (ISOGG) maintains a detailed Y-DNA phylogenetic tree of humankind. There is a similar tree based on MT-DNA maintained at Erasmus MC in the

Netherlands. The trees are updated as new data become available.

A shortened version of the Y-DNA tree appears in chart 5.5. It shows the key markers, such as M9 and M20, on the left side. The twenty top-level haplogroups from A to T appear on the right side.

DNA Tests

Although several different tests are used in DNA studies, there are only two of interest for our purposes: Y-DNA and MT-DNA.

- Y-DNA tests are available only to males, because the genes are passed from father to son on the Y chromosome. The tests examine either STRs or SNPs on the Y chromosome, and they provide a haplotype that is used to predict the haplogroup. Of the two tests, the SNP test is more precise.
- MT-DNA tests are available to both males and females. The tests only examine the matrilineal ancestry using DNA in the

mitochondria. A male using this test would be a terminus because his children would not share his MT-DNA.

Because paternity cannot be determined for females through Y-DNA tests, a close male family member (father or brother) can be tested to determine deep ancestry.

What DNA Tests Do Not Tell Us

The tests do not produce a family tree. They cannot tell who one's great-great-great-grandfather was or which town or village he came from. The tests can tell if two people are related but cannot determine the degree of relationship (for example, if they are first cousins or fifth cousins). The tests can reveal information only about a small percentage of the genome.

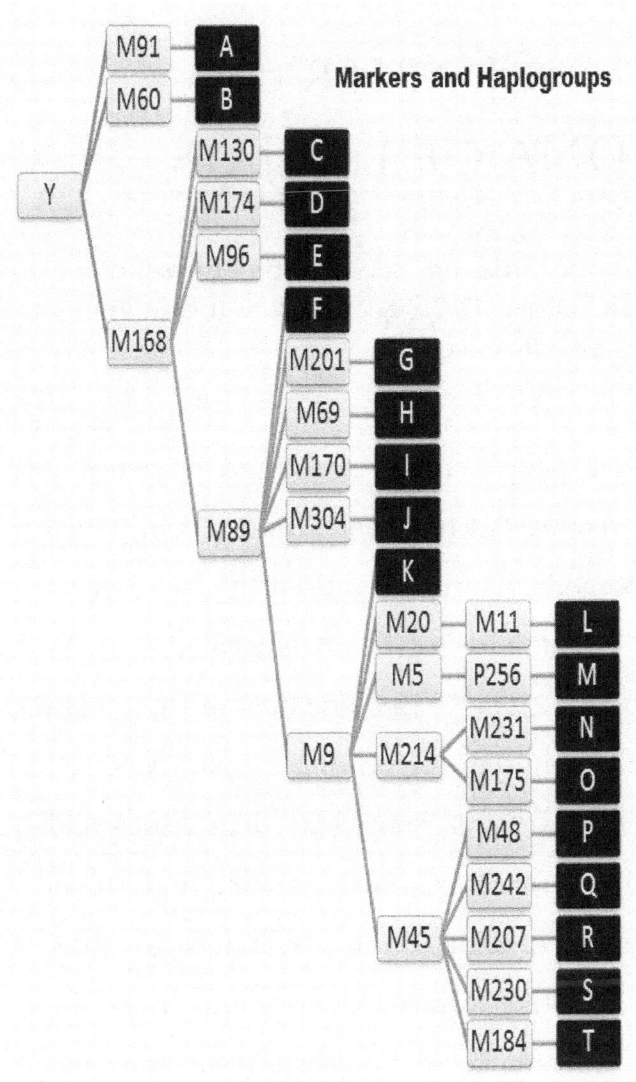

5.5 Phylogenetic Tree

Chapter 6
DNA of the Jats

> Written records go back to the dawn of written history. DNA goes back to the dawn of human existence.
> --George Church

All people living today are genetically connected to a man who lived in Africa more than one hundred thousand years ago. This great ancestor is often termed the "Y-chromosomal Adam." Descendants of this man from the present-day region of Ethiopia dispersed in different directions. Some stayed in Africa and moved to different parts of the region, and others shifted to the Arabian Peninsula and began their journeys to other lands. One group from the Arabian Peninsula took the coastal route through India, Myanmar, and Malaysia to Australia. Another group moved north into Central

Asia and eventually toward China, Siberia, and Europe. A related group went west toward the Mediterranean and Europe. All these journeys were undertaken on foot, possibly with the help of some animals after they were domesticated. There is no evidence of ocean-sailing technology that long ago.

These migrations did not occur in straight lines. People moved to a new area and stayed there, continued onward and dispersed in different directions, or returned to an earlier area. They stayed with their own clans, or merged with communities that were already established. By living in different climates, eating different types of food, and breeding with people who were already there—thereby mixing the genes—their color, size, and physiognomy changed. These ancestors are identified by their haplogroups.

Major Jat Haplogroups

Although there are twenty major Y-DNA haplogroups (designated with the letters A to T), not all of them are observed in the Indian subcontinent in significant numbers. For example, haplogroups A and B are primarily seen in Africa. Haplogroup A is believed to be the original haplogroup of the Y-chromosomal Adam. Similarly, there are haplogroups that are more prevalent in other parts of the world. A few haplogroups are prominent only in Europe. For example, haplogroup I and its subgroups are predominantly found in northwestern Europe, and haplogroup N is predominantly found in northeastern Europe. Although haplogroup Q is primarily associated with Native American populations, with the vast immigrations that have taken place over the years, North America now has a wide representation of different haplogroups.[1]

A comprehensive Y-Chromosome Haplotype Reference Database (YHRD) is maintained at YHRD.org in Berlin. As of this writing, laboratories and institutions from around the world have contributed over 130,000 haplotypes of different population groups for this database. For the purposes of our study, 1,291 haplotypes from this database were analyzed, representing fifty-two communities from the Indian subcontinent. This sample contained ninety-four haplotypes from the communities of Jat Sikhs in Punjab and Jats in Haryana.

All haplotypes in the sample population were processed through Whit Athey's Haplogroup Predictor, a software program, and the results were sorted in a database. Only the predominant top-level haplogroups were identified. The subhaplogroups or subclades were not used. All outcomes are for paternal lines.

The overall distribution of haplogroups is shown in chart 6.1. The results are rough approximations of what would be found in the total population of the communities. Of the twenty major haplogroups, six were identified as having significant representation in the sample of Jats, as shown in chart 6.2.

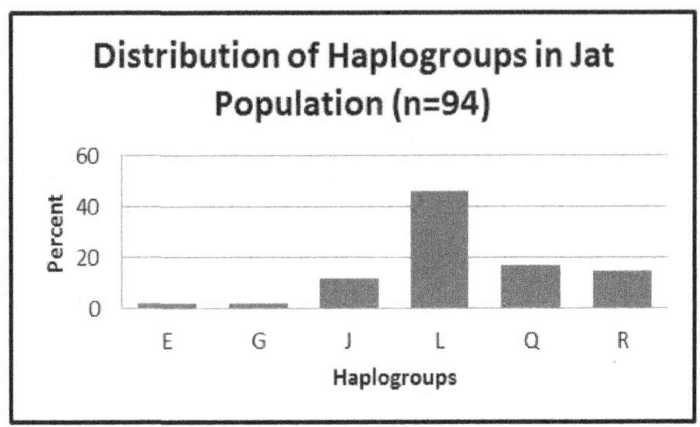

6.1 Distribution

The low to high values in the range are based on a confidence level of 95 percent and a margin of error of plus or minus 10.1 percent for this sample. In other words, if this survey is conducted one hundred times among a similar group of people (i.e., 94 x 100; 9,400 people in total), in ninety-five surveys, the results are expected to fall between the low to high values in the range.

For example, the representation of haplogroup "L" in ninety-five of these surveys is expected to fall between 39 to 59 percent. Actually, the percent representation is really not very important for our purposes here because we are primarily interested in identifying the ancestral origins or haplogroups of these people.

Haplogroups in Jat Population							
Community	Punjab		Haryana		Total		Range
Haplogroup	Nbr	%	Nbr	%	Nbr	%	%
E	2	5	0	0	2	2	0 - 12%
G	0	0	2	4	2	2	0 - 12%
J	5	12	7	13	12	13	3 - 23%
L	20	48	26	50	46	49	39 - 59%
Q	2	5	15	29	17	18	8 - 28%
R	13	31	2	4	15	16	6 - 26%
Total	42	100	52	100	94	100	

6.2 Jat haplogroups

Based on the data, the basic conclusion is that the Jat population in India has at least six major lines of ancestry as reflected by haplogroups E, G, J, L, Q, and R. For lack of data, the Muslim Jats of Pakistan are not included in this survey. It is likely that another few haplogroups may emerge if a larger population and the Muslim Jat community is surveyed. But the ones identified in this survey appear to be the predominant ones. The approximate geographic origins of the six haplogroups are shown in the following map of India and surrounding regions. The origins of three key early markers (M9, M89, and M168) for the ancestors of these haplogroups are also shown.

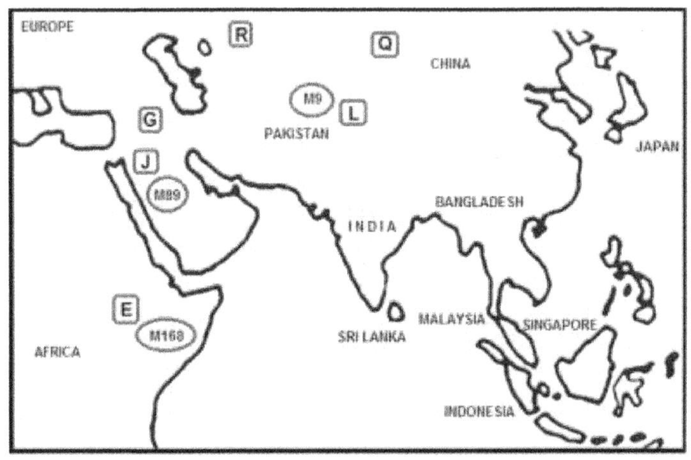

6.3 Geographic Origins of Jat Haplogroups

Shared DNA

The six haplogroups identified for the Jats are not unique to them. The research study in my previous book *Before India: Exploring Your Ancestry with DNA* revealed that the Jats share an underlying genetic unity with several other ethnic communities in the Indian subcontinent. As shown in the following chart 6.4, a survey of 689 people identified several other ethnic communities in India with representation in the same haplogroups as the Jats.

INDIA: REPRESENTATION SIX MAJOR HAPLOGROUPS						
Community	E	G	J	L	Q	R
Andhra Pradesh, Brahmin	√			√		√
Gujarat, Bhil		√	√	√	√	√
Haryana, Jat		√	√	√	√	√
Himacha Pradesh, Gaddi		√	√			√
Himachal Pradesh, Gujjar			√			√
Himachal Pradesh, Saraswat Brahmin			√	√	√	√
Jammu, Saraswat Brahmin			√	√	√	√
Jharkhand, Sakaldwipi Brahmin						√
Karnatka, Brahmin	√		√	√	√	√
Kashmir, Saraswat Brahmin			√	√	√	
Madhya Pradesh, Gond		√		√		√
Madhya Pradesh, Kanyakubja Brahmin		√	√		√	√
Maharashtra, Konkanastha Brahmin	√		√	√	√	√
Maharashtra, Mahadev Koli	√		√	√	√	
Punjab, Balmiki			√	√	√	
Punjab, Jat Sikh	√		√	√	√	√
Punjab, Saraswat Brahmin			√	√	√	√
Rajasthan, Saraswat Brahmin			√	√		√
Southern India, Tamil	√	√	√	√	√	
Tamil Nadu, Iyengar			√	√		√
Tamil Nadu, Kuruman			√	√	√	
Tripura, Riang			√	√	√	√
Tripura, Tripuri			√	√	√	
Uttar Pradesh, Afridi Pathan	√	√	√	√		√
West Bengal, Dhimal			√	√	√	
West Bengal, Paliya			√	√		√
West Bengal, Rabha				√	√	√
West Bengal, Rajbanshi			√	√	√	√

6.4 Ethnic Communities in India

A survey of 602 people in Bangla Desh, Pakistan, and Sri Lanka revealed the same thing, namely, that many other ethnic communities share the same haplogroups as the Jats. In short, members of all these communities in the same haplogroups have the same most recent common ancestors.

ADJACENT COUNTRIES : REPRESENTATION SIX MAJOR HAPLOGROUPS						
Community	E	G	J	L	Q	R
Bangladesh, Bangladeshi			√	√	√	√
Bangladesh, Dinajpur (Santal)					√	
Bangladesh, Tangali (Garo)			√	√	√	
Pakistan, Baltistan (Balti)			√			√
Pakistan, Chitral (Kalash)		√	√	√		
Pakistan, Hazara (Hazara)					√	√
Pakistan, Hunza (Burusho)			√	√	√	√
Pakistan, Kalat (Brahui)		√	√			√
Pakistan, Kashmir (Kashmiri)			√			√
Pakistan, Khyber Pakhtunkhwa (Pathan)			√	√		√
Pakistan, Makran Coast (Baloch)	√	√	√	√		√
Pakistan, Makran Coast (Negroid)	√		√		√	√
Pakistan, Mastung (Baloch)	√		√	√		√
Pakistan, Northern Sindh (Sindhi)			√	√		√
Pakistan, Pathan	√			√		√
Pakistan, Punjabi	√	√	√	√		√
Pakistan, Western Sindh (Parsi)			√	√		√
Sri Lanka, Sri Lankan	√	√		√		√

6.5 Ethnic Communities in Adjacent Countries

CHAPTER 7
ANCESTRAL GROUPS

The greatest history book ever written is the one hidden in our DNA.
—Spencer Wells

The six major Y-DNA haplogroups for Jats are described in more detail in the following pages. The haplogroup's ancestral line on the phylogenetic tree is identified. There is a brief description of where the haplogroup originated.

The ancestral line for each haplogroup can be traced on the phylogenetic tree provided in chapter 5. The age of the M168 mutation on the phylogenetic tree has been estimated to be forty thousand years, and it represents the last ancestor of all non-African Y chromosomes.[1] Some other ethnic communities from the Indian subcontinent that belong to the same haplogroup are also identified.

HAPLOGROUP "E"

Ancestral Line on the Phylogenetic Tree:

M168 → M96

This haplogroup originated in northeast Africa some thirty to forty thousand years ago. The group is found in all regions in Africa and exists in some populations in the Middle East, Europe, and Asia. One of its subclades that may have evolved in the Middle East is predominantly found along the Mediterranean coast.

Members of this group may have emerged from what is known as the "Middle East clan." The group is also present in North America, primarily because of the slave trade that brought Africans to America.

The following ethnic communities, including the Jats, are represented in this haplogroup (see charts 6.4 and 6.5).

- India, Andhra Pradesh, Brahmin
- India, Karnatka, Brahmin
- India, Maharashtra, Konkanastha Brahmin
- India, Maharashtra, Mahadev Koll
- ***India, Punjab, Jat Sikh***
- India, Southern India, Tamil
- India, Uttar Pradesh, Afridi Pathan

- Pakistan, Makran Coast, Baloch
- Pakistan, Makran Coast, Negroid
- Pakistan, Mastung, Baloch
- Pakistan, Pathan
- Pakistan, Punjabi
- Sri Lanka, Sri Lankan

HAPLOGROUP "G"

Ancestral Line on the Phylogenetic Tree:

M168 → M89 → M201

The M201 marker emerged about thirty thousand years ago somewhere along the eastern edge of the Middle East or in the Himalayan foothills of Pakistan or India.

This haplogroup is widely distributed in Europe, northern and western Asia, northern Africa, the Middle East, and parts of India. There are indications that members of this group were engaged in farming in the Indus Valley at one time.

The body of Ötzi the Iceman found in the Italian Alps in 1991 belongs to a subclade of this group.

Another subclade is a distinctive genetic marker of Ashkenazi Jews.

In a 2010 study of forty-five Cochin Jews from South India, it was found that none belonged to this group, but 6.5 percent of thirty-one Bene Israel Jews from Mumbai were in this group.[2]

The following ethnic communities, including the Jats, are represented in this haplogroup (see charts 6.4 and 6.5).

- India, Gujarat, Bhil
- ***India, Haryana, Jat***
- India, Himachal Pradesh, Gaddi
- India, Madhya Pradesh, Gond
- India, Madhya Pradesh, Kanyakubja Brahmin
- India, Southern India, Tamil
- India, Uttar Pradesh, Afridi Pathan
- Pakistan, Chitral, Kalash
- Pakistan, Kalat, Brahui
- Pakistan, Makran Coast, Baloch
- Pakistan, Punjabi
- Sri Lanka, Sri Lankan

HAPLOGROUP "J"

Ancestral Line on the Phylogenetic Tree:

M168 → M89 → M304

The man carrying the M304 mutation was born around fifteen thousand years ago in the Middle East area known as the Fertile Crescent, which includes Israel, the West Bank, Jordan, Lebanon, Syria, and Iraq. There is a dominant Arabic lineage. This group and its subclades are found predominantly around the coast of the Mediterranean, the Middle East, North Africa, and Ethiopia. One subclade has a frequency of about 30 percent among the Jewish people. Middle Eastern traders carried this marker into various regions, including Europe, Central Asia, India, and Pakistan.[3]

The following ethnic communities, including the Jats, are represented in this haplogroup (see charts 6.4 and 6.5).

- Bangladesh, Bangladeshi
- Bangladesh, Tangali, Garo
- India, Gujarat, Bhil

- ***India, Haryana, Jat***
- India, Himachal Pradesh, Gaddi
- India, Himachal Pradesh, Gujjar
- India, Himachal Pradesh, Saraswat Brahmin
- India, Jammu, Saraswat Brahmin
- India, Karnatka, Brahmin
- India, Kashmir, Saraswat Brahmin
- India, Madhya Pradesh, Kanyakubja Brahmin
- India, Maharashtra, Konkanastha Brahmin
- India, Maharashtra, Mahadev Koll
- India, Punjab, Balmiki
- ***India, Punjab, Jat Sikh***
- India, Punjab, Saraswat Brahmin
- India, Rajasthan, Saraswat Brahmin
- India, Southern India, Tamil
- India, Tamil Nadu, Iyengar
- India, Tamil Nadu, Kuruman
- India, Tripura, Riang
- India, Tripura, Tripuri
- India, Uttar Pradesh, Afridi Pathan
- India, West Bengal, Dhimal
- India, West Bengal, Paliya
- India, West Bengal, Rajbanshi
- Pakistan, Baltistan, Balti
- Pakistan, Chitral, Kalash
- Pakistan, Hunza, Burusho
- Pakistan, Kalat, Brahui
- Pakistan, Kashmir, Kashmiri

- Pakistan, Khyber Pakhtunkhwa, Yousafzai Pathan
- Pakistan, Makran Coast, Baloch
- Pakistan, Makran Coast, Negroid
- Pakistan, Mastung, Baloch
- Pakistan, Northern Sindh, Sindhi
- Pakistan, Punjab, Punjabi
- Pakistan, Western Sindh, Parsi

HAPLOGROUP "L"

Ancestral Line on Phylogenetic Tree:

M168 → M89 → M9 → M20 → M11

The ancestors of this group arrived in India twenty-five to thirty thousand years ago. This group is part of the Eurasian clan that migrated south once it reached the mountainous Pamir Knot region (Hindu Kush, the Tian Shan, and the Himalayas) in Tajikistan. The group and its subclades are found primarily in India, Pakistan, Afghanistan, Tajikistan, and Uzbekistan. It is found in low frequencies in the Middle East, parts of the Caucasus, and a few European countries. The group may be one of the creators of the Indus Valley Civilization.[4]

The following ethnic communities, including the Jats, are represented in this haplogroup (see charts 6.4 and 6.5).

- Bangladesh, Bangladeshi
- Bangladesh, Tangali, Garo
- India, Andhra Pradesh, Brahmin
- India, Gujarat, Bhil
- ***India, Haryana, Jat***
- India, Himachal Pradesh, Saraswat Brahmin
- India, Jammu, Saraswat Brahmin
- India, Karnatka, Brahmin
- India, Kashmir, Saraswat Brahmin
- India, Madhya Pradesh, Gond
- India, Maharashtra, Konkanastha Brahmin
- India, Maharashtra, Mahadev Koll
- India, Punjab, Balmiki
- ***India, Punjab, Jat Sikh***
- India, Punjab, Saraswat Brahmin
- India, Rajasthan, Saraswat Brahmin
- India, Southern India, Tamil
- India, Tamil Nadu, Iyengar
- India, Tamil Nadu, Kuruman
- India, Tripura, Riang
- India, Tripura, Tripuri
- India, Uttar Pradesh, Afridi Pathan
- India, West Bengal, Dhimal
- India, West Bengal, Paliya
- India, West Bengal, Rabha
- India, West Bengal, Rajbanshi
- Pakistan, Chitral, Kalash

- Pakistan, Hunza, Burusho
- Pakistan, Khyber Pakhtunkhwa, Yousafzai Pathan
- Pakistan, Makran Coast, Baloch
- Pakistan, Mastung, Baloch
- Pakistan, Northern Sindh, Sindhi
- Pakistan, Pathan
- Pakistan, Punjab, Punjabi
- Pakistan, Western Sindh, Parsi
- Sri Lanka, Sri Lankan

HAPLOGROUP "Q"

Ancestral Line on the Phylogenetic Tree:

M168 → M89 → M9 → M45 → M242

The man with the M242 mutation was born in Siberia fifteen to twenty thousand years ago. His descendants traveled through northern Eurasia toward the east and crossed what was then the Beringia passage connecting Siberia and Alaska. They were the first people to reach North America.[5] Scientists have estimated that as few as twenty people may have founded the native population of the Americas.[6]

Some members of the group moved to the western and southern areas. The descendants, known as the Siberian clan, are found in Siberia, China, and India. The group is also linked to the Huns, Mongols, and Turkic people.

The following ethnic communities, including the Jats, are represented in this haplogroup (see charts 6.4 and 6.5).

- Bangladesh, Bangladeshi
- Bangladesh, Dinajpur, Santal
- Bangladesh, Tangali, Garo
- India, Gujarat, Bhil
- ***India, Haryana, Jat***
- India, Himachal Pradesh, Saraswat Brahmin
- India, Jammu, Saraswat Brahmin
- India, Karnatka, Brahmin
- India, Kashmir, Saraswat Brahmin
- India, Madhya Pradesh, Kanyakubja Brahmin
- India, Maharashtra, Konkanastha Brahmin
- India, Maharashtra, Mahadev Koll
- India, Punjab, Balmiki
- ***India, Punjab, Jat Sikh***
- India, Punjab, Saraswat Brahmin
- India, Southern India, Tamil
- India, Tamil Nadu, Kuruman
- India, Tripura, Riang

- India, Tripura, Tripuri
- India, West Bengal, Dhimal
- India, West Bengal, Rabha
- India, West Bengal, Rajbanshi
- Pakistan, Hazara, Hazara
- Pakistan, Hunza, Burusho
- Pakistan, Makran Coast, Negroid

HAPLOGROUP "R"

Ancestral Line on the Phylogenetic Tree:

M168 → M89 → M9 → M45 → M207

After arriving in Central Asia, the descendants of the man carrying the M207 mutation split into two groups. One group went west toward Europe, and the other headed south to arrive in India about ten thousand years ago.

Branches of this group are found in all parts of Europe, the British Isles, and the Americas after recent migrations. A branch of these people is believed to be the first speakers of the Indo-European languages and responsible for the domestication of the horse around 3000 BCE. This is one of the largest haplogroups in India and Pakistan.

The following ethnic communities, including the Jats, are represented in this haplogroup (see charts 6.4 and 6.5).

- Bangladesh, Bangladeshi
- India, Andhra Pradesh, Brahmin
- India, Gujarat, Bhil
- ***India, Haryana, Jat***
- India, Himachal Pradesh, Gaddi
- India, Himachal Pradesh, Gujjar
- India, Himachal Pradesh, Saraswat Brahmin
- India, Jammu, Saraswat Brahmin
- India, Jharkhand, Sakaldwipi Brahmin
- India, Karnatka, Brahmin
- India, Madhya Pradesh, Gond
- India, Madhya Pradesh, Kanyakubja Brahmin
- India, Maharashtra, Konkanastha Brahmin
- ***India, Punjab, Jat Sikh***
- India, Punjab, Saraswat Brahmin
- India, Rajasthan, Saraswat Brahmin
- India, Tamil Nadu, Iyengar
- India, Tripura, Riang
- India, Uttar Pradesh, Afridi Pathan
- India, West Bengal, Paliya
- India, West Bengal, Rabha
- India, West Bengal, Rajbanshi

- Pakistan, Baltistan, Balti
- Pakistan, Hazara, Hazara
- Pakistan, Hunza, Burusho
- Pakistan, Kalat, Brahui
- Pakistan, Kashmir, Kashmiri
- Pakistan, Khyber Pakhtunkhwa, Yousafzai Pathan
- Pakistan, Makran Coast, Baloch
- Pakistan, Makran Coast, Negroid
- Pakistan, Mastung, Baloch
- Pakistan, Northern Sindh, Sindhi
- Pakistan, Pathan
- Pakistan, Punjabi
- Pakistan, Western Sindh, Parsi
- Sri Lanka, Sri Lankan

CHAPTER 8
CONCLUSION

If everybody is thinking alike, then somebody isn't thinking.
—General George Patton

The states of Punjab in the north and Kerala in the south are located in the opposite corners of India and separated by about 1,500 miles (2,400 kilometers). The communities of Jat Sikhs from Punjab and the Ezhavas from Kerala have distinctly different cultures in terms of language, religion, cuisine, and history. In 2010, a study of the paternal lineage of the Ezhava community was conducted at the Sree Buddha College of Engineering in Kerala. It revealed that of the 104 haplotypes tested, ten were identical to the Jat Sikh population and four to the Turkish population. Based on the genotype, the Ezhavas showed more resemblance to Jat Sikh and Turkish populations than to East Asians.[1]

Other remarkable linkages appear among the different communities. Even with the traditional endogamous practices of people in the Indian subcontinent, who generally marry within their own castes and communities, it cannot be said that their genes have remained relatively pure over time. Perhaps endogamy was not as prevalent in the distant past when the populations were much smaller.

Vincent Smith was an Irish-born Indologist and historian who lived and worked in India between 1871 and 1900 as an officer in the Indian Civil Service. He wrote several books about the country and said the following about the people of India:

> In my judgment it is absolutely impossible to decide who were the earliest inhabitants of India, either in the north or the south, or to ascertain whence they came. Nor can we

> say what their bodily type was. The modern population of India almost everywhere is far too mixed...The mixture of races on Indian soil was going on for countless ages before any history was recorded, and it is hopeless now to unravel the different lines of descent.[2]

About a hundred years later, DNA science can unravel the ancestral lines of descent. But the population of the subcontinent is indeed very mixed. After seeing the results of many research studies, Dr. Ramasamy Pitchappan, who headed National Geographic's Genographic Project in India, also says that "no caste is 'pure.'"[3] The research shows that the Jats, as a group, are no exception.

According to the research study described in this book, the Jats have at least six ancestral lines that go back ten to forty thousand years. The entire population of India in 10000 BCE is mathematically estimated to have been less than one million.[4] On this basis, in 40000 BCE, India was a newfound sparsely populated land with very few people. For perspective, this is about the time when people were moving into or living in the Bhimbetka caves of Madhya Pradesh, and prior to the emergence of the Indus Valley Civilization.

The main conclusions about the ancestry of Jats are summarized in the following chart:

Ancestral Roots of the Jats		
HAPLOGROUP	MARKER	ORIGINS
E	M96	Northeast Africa
G	M201	Eastern edge of the Middle East
J	M304	Fertile Crescent (Mesopotamia, the land in and around the Tigris and Euphrates rivers)
L	M11	Pamir Knot region (Hindu Kush, Tian Shan, Himalayas) in Tajikistan
Q	M242	Siberia (North Asia)
R	M207	Central Asia (from the Caspian Sea to border of western China)

As explained earlier, the Jats are not the only ones with these origins. There are people in many other ethnic communities of the Indian subcontinent that have the same most recent common ancestors with the same markers.

The research study in this book and other similar studies reveal an underlying genetic unity that cuts across several ethnic communities in the Indian subcontinent. That makes 'race' a meaningless concept. Therefore, any historical references to the Jats being descendants of any one specific group of people (like the Aryans, Scythians, Medes, Scandinavians, and so on) cannot be scientifically substantiated.

Additional studies may reveal that the Jats have a few more lines of ancestry. A DNA study of Muslim Jats in Pakistan will add value to this study. As explained earlier, the Jats separated into three communities—Hindu, Muslim, and Sikh—only during about the last one thousand years. It is a reasonably safe assumption that many Jats in India and Pakistan belong to the same haplogroups.

To conclude, the ancestors of Jats and other ethnic communities of the Indian subcontinent go back many thousand years. Over time, these people came from many different directions as stragglers, nomads, hunter-gatherers, peaceful migraters, and fierce invaders. They mixed and merged with people who had arrived earlier. Because of the need for fellowship and common good, they formed new clans and communities, and created their own distinct languages, cultures, and cuisines. Gradually, a colorful tapestry of many different ethnic communities emerged.

As explained in this book, our written history is less than twenty-five hundred years old. For any time before this period we need to use evidence-based information and hard facts from the fields of archaeology, anthropology, and science. Recent developments in DNA science have started to reveal convincingly where our deep ancestry lies.

GLOSSARY

allele. A variant form of a gene at a particular locus (location) on a chromosome. It represents the number of repeats in an STR marker (see *short tandem repeats*).

anthropology. The study of humans, their origins, classification, and relationship of races.

archaeology. The study of material remains of past human life.

base pair. The two bases that form the ladder of the DNA molecule. The bases are the letters that spell out the genetic code. The letters are A (adenine), T (thymine), G (guanine), and C (cytosine). A always pairs with T, and G always pairs with C.

BCE. Before the current era (same as BC).

CE. Of the common era (same as AD).

cell. The smallest independent unit of living matter.

chromosomes. The long, threadlike strands of DNA on which genes are found.

clade and **subclade.** A subhaplogroup.

consanguinity. A shared blood relationship.

cuneiform. The written language that was invented in Mesopotamia (in Sumer, present Iraq) around 3200 BCE.

deoxyribonucleic acid (DNA). The molecule inside the nucleus of a cell that carries the organism's genetic information.

DYS number. The genetic markers on the Y chromosome. D stands for DNA, Y for Y chromosome, and S for a unique segment of DNA.

double helix. The shape of DNA, which resembles a spiral staircase or twisted ladder.

gene. The segment of DNA that is the basic unit of heredity and is passed from parent to offspring.

genealogy. Tracing human lineage through DNA testing and comparison of haplotypes.

genetics. The science of genes, heredity, and variation in living organisms.

haplogroup. A population group descended from a common ancestor based on SNP mutations (see *single nucleotide polymorphism*). The haplogroups are assigned alphanumeric labels that can be shown on a phylogenetic or haplogroup tree. It is like the branch on a tree.

haplotype. The set of results obtained from multiple markers located on a single chromosome. It is like the leaf on a branch.

locus. A location on a chromosome identified by a marker.

marker. An identifiable physical location on a chromosome that varies between individuals. It is used with allele values to describe an individual's haplotype.

Mitochondrial Eve. The most recent common female ancestor of all humans.

most recent common ancestor (MRCA). The shared ancestor of two or more people who represents their most recent link.

MT-DNA. Genetic material passed from mothers to their children, but only females are able to pass it on.

mutation. A permanent structural alteration in DNA.

nucleotide. A DNA building block that contains a base or half of a staircase step on the double helix.

phylogeny. Shown as a tree that illustrates the relations and development of all species.

replication. The process by which two DNA strands separate and create a new strand. During reproduction, the double helix unwinds and duplicates itself to pass on genetic information to the next generation.

single nucleotide polymorphism (SNP). Small changes that create a person's unique DNA pattern.

short tandem repeat (STR). The patterns in the DNA sequence that repeat. The allele values in the haplotype represent the number of repeats.

X and Y chromosomes. The chromosomes that determine sex. Females have two X chromosomes, and males have one X and one Y chromosome.

Y-Adam. The most recent common male ancestor of all humans.

Y-DNA. Genetic material passed from fathers to sons essentially unaltered except for occasional mutations.

ACKNOWLEDGMENTS

Remembering the adage "A picture is worth a thousand words," I have used several pictures, maps, charts, and graphs. Unless stated otherwise, the maps and photographs are in the public domain and used courtesy of Wikimedia Commons. The charts and graphs were created in-house.

The map depicting migrations out of Africa in chapter 2 was proposed by Dr. Naruya Saitou at the (Japanese) National Institute for Genetics, and it originally appeared on the Kyushu Museum website in Japan.

The illustration of the human cell in chapter 5 is used with the permission of FamilyTreeDNA.com. In the same chapter, the illustrations of chromosomes, the double helix, and the human gene are used courtesy of the US National Library of Medicine.

The data maintained by YHRD.org was invaluable in conducting my research about Indian haplogroups. Whit Athey's Haplogroup Predictor made the job easier.

The definitions of haplogroups are summarized from Charles Kerchner's website, kerchner.com, the website "Y Haplogroups" at Nechbet.com, and the books *Trace Your Roots with DNA: Using Genetic Tests to Explore Your Family Tree* by Megan Smolenyak and Ann Turner, and *Deep Ancestry* by Spencer Wells.

NOTES

PREFACE

1. Ujagar Singh Mahil, *Antiquity of Jat Race* (New Delhi: Atma Ram & Sons, 1955).

INTRODUCTION

1. Government of India, *Census of India*, Vol. 1, Pt. 2 (1933, 1931).

2. Saubhadra Chatterji, "Government Turns Focus on Jat Quota," *Hindustan Times*, January 14, 2012.

3. David G. Mahal, *Before India: Exploring Your Ancestry with DNA* (Pacific Palisades, CA: DGM Associates, 2014).

CHAPTER 1: THE WRITTEN WORD

1. Dinesh C. Sharma, "Indians Are Not Descendants of Aryans, Says New Study," *India Today*, December 2011.

2. Martha Congleton Howell and Walter Prevenier, *Reliable Sources: An Introduction to Historical Methods* (Ithaca, NY: Cornell University Press, 2001).

3. Herodotus, Aubrey de Selincourt (translator), *The Histories* (London: Penguin Books, 1954).

4. "Takshila: World's First University," *Incredible India*, February 26, 2009, http://incredibleindia.blogspot.com.

5. "Herodotus," *Ancient History Encyclopedia*, http://www.ancient.eu/herodotus/.

6. Plutarch, Lionel Pearson (translator), *Moralia XI: On the Malice of Herodotus* (Cambridge, MA: Harvard University Press, Loeb Classical Library, 1965).

7. Alan Fildes and Joann Fletcher, *Alexander the Great: Son of the Gods* (Los Angeles: Getty Publications, 2002).

CHAPTER 2: FIRST ARRIVALS

1. Luigi Luca Cavalli-Sforza and Francesco Cavalli-Sforza, *The Great Human Diasporas: The History of Diversity and Evolution* (New York: Perseus Books, 1996).

2. John Roach, "Massive Genetic Study Supports 'Out of Africa' Theory," *National Geographic News*, February 21, 2008.

3. Donald C. Johanson, "Origins of Modern Humans: Multiregional or Out of Africa?" American Institute of Biological Sciences (May 2001), http://www.actionbioscience.org.

4. David Whitehouse, "When Humans Faced Extinction," BBC News Online, http://news.bbc.co.uk/2/hi/science/nature/2975862.stm.

5. Tim Jones, "Mount Toba Eruption—Ancient Humans Unscathed, Study Claims" (July 2007), http://www.anthropology.net.

6. Paul Hamaker, "Sri Lankan 'Balangoda Man' Dated to 37,000 Years Ago," Examiner.com, http://www.examiner.com/article/sri-lankan-balangoda-man-dated-to-37-000-years-ago.

7. Allen Worwood and Brittany Shamess, "The Great Human Migration," Madurai Messenger, July 2010.

CHAPTER 3: NEW MIGRATIONS

1. William F. Fisher, *Toward Sustainable Development: Struggling over India's Narmada River* (Armonk, NY: M. E. Sharpe, 1995).

2. World Heritage Sites, "Rock Shelters of Bhimbetka," Archaeological Survey of India, http://asi.nic.in.

3. Nivedita Khandekar, "Indus Valley 2,000 Years Older Than Thought," *Hindustan Times*, November 4, 2012.

4. David R. Harris, *The Origins and Spread of Agriculture and Pastoralism in Eurasia* (New York: Routledge, 1996).

5. Gregory L. Possehl, *Oxford Companion to Archaeology, Mehrgarh* (Oxford: Oxford University Press, 1996).

6. "Mehrgarh Culture," Wikibooks.org, http://en.wikibooks.org/wiki/Ancient_History/Indian_subcontinent/Mehrgarh_Culture.

7. A. Coppa et al., "Early Neolithic Tradition of Dentistry: Flint Tips Were Surprisingly Effective for Drilling Tooth Enamel in a Prehistoric Population," *Nature*, April 6, 2006.

8. Colin McEvedy and Richard Jones, *Atlas of World Population History* (New York: Puffin-Penguin Books, 1978).

9. Michael Wood, *India* (New York: Basic Books, 2007).

10. J. P. Mallory, *In Search of the Indo-Europeans: Language, Archaeology, and Myth* (London: Thames & Hudson, 1989).

11. Osmond Bopearachchi, "Monnaies Greco-Bactriennes et Indo-Grecques," *Wikepedia*, Bibliotheque Nationale (1991), http://en.wikipedia.org/wiki/Osmund_Bopearachchi.

12. Krishna Chandra Sagar, *Foreign Influence on Ancient India* (New Delhi: Northern Book Centre, 1992).

13. "The White Huns—The Hephthalites," The Silkroad Foundation, Saratoga, California, http://www.silkroad.com/artl/heph.shtml.

14. Hillary Mayell, "Genghis Khan a Prolific Lover, DNA Data Implies," *National Geographic News*, February 14, 2003.

15. B. S. Ahloowalia, *Invasion of the Genes: Genetic Heritage of India* (New York: Eloquent Books, 2009).

CHAPTER 4: COUNTING ANCESTORS

1. Brian Pears, "Our Ancestors, Conceptions, Misconceptions and a Paradox," http://www.bpears.org.uk

2. Alan Boyle, "All Europeans Are Related If You Go Back Just 1,000 Years, Scientists Say," NBC News, May 7, 2013,

CHAPTER 5: GENES AND GENEALOGY

1. Gina Smith, *The Genomics Age: How DNA Technology Is Transforming the Way We Live and Who We Are* (New York: AMACOM, 2004).

2. "Pharmacogenomics Program," The Mayo Clinic, http://mayoresearch.mayo.edu/center-for-individualized-medicine/pharmacogenomics.asp.

3. Alan Boyle,"Scientists Say Otzi the Iceman Has Living Relatives, 5,300 Years Later," NBC.com, October 14, 2013

4. "DNA Wars: How the Cell Strikes Back to Avoid Disease after Attacks on DNA," MIT OpenCourseWare, Massachussetts Institute of Technology, http://ocw.mit.edu/courses/biology/2013

5. Spencer Wells, *Deep Ancestry* (Washington DC: National Geographic Society, 2007).

6. Megan Smolenyak and Ann Turner, *Trace Your Roots with DNA* (Emmaus, PA: Rodale Books, 2004).

Chapter 6: DNA of the Jats

1. Spencer Wells, *The Journey of Man: A Genetic Odyssey* (Princeton, NJ: Princeton University Press, 2002).

Chapter 7: Ancestral Groups

1. P. A. Underhill et al., "The Phylogeography of Y Chromosome Binary Haplotypes and the Origins of Modern Human Populations," *Annals of Human Genetics* 65 (2001)

2. D. Behar, "The Genome-Wide Structure of the Jewish People," *Nature*, July 2010.

3. Charles Kerchner, "YDNA Haplogroup Descriptions and Information Links," http://www.kerchner.com/haplogroups-ydna.htm.

4. S. Sengupta et al., "Polarity and Temporality of High-Resolution Y-Chromosome Distributions in India Identify Both Indigenous and Exogenous Expansions and Reveal Minor Genetic Influence of Central Asian Pastoralists," *American Journal of Human Genetics* (2006), 202–221.

5. Alok Jha, "Humans Arrived in North America 2,500 Years Earlier Than Thought," *Guardian*, March 24, 2011.

6. Dennis Liu, "Using DNA to Trace Human Migration," Howard Hughes Medical Institute, http://www.hhmi.org/biointeractive/using-dna-trace-human-migration.

CHAPTER 8: CONCLUSION

1. S. P. Nair, A. Geetha, and C. Jagannath, "Y-Short Tandem Repeat Haplotype and Paternal Lineage of the Ezhava Population of Kerala, South India," National Library of Medicine, June 2011, http://www.ncbi.nlm.nih.gov/pubmed/?term=Geetha+A.+Nair.

2. Vincent A. Smith, *The Oxford History of India from the Earliest Times to the End of 1911* (Oxford: Oxford University Press, 1928).

3. Ramasamy Pitchappan, email message to author, July 16, 2012.

4. Colin McEvedy and Richard Jones, *Atlas of World Population History* (New York: Puffin-Penguin Books, 1978).

Resources

Suggested Reading

Cavalli-Sforza, Luigi Luca, and Francesco Cavalli-Sforza. *The Great Human Diasporas: The History of Diversity and Evolution.* Reading, MA: Perseus Books, 1995.

Fitzpatrick, Colleen and Andrew Yeiser. *DNA and Genealogy*. Fountain Valley, CA: Rice Book Press, 2005.

Wells, Spencer. *The Journey of Man: A Genetic Odyssey.* Princeton, NJ: Princeton University Press, 2003.

DNA Testing Laboratories

23andme, http://www.23andme.com

Ancestry.com, http://www.Ancestry.com

BritainsDNA, http://www.britainsdna.com

FamilyTreeDNA, http://www.familytreedna.com

GenTrace, http://www.dnafamilycheck.com

National Geographic Genographic Project,
https://genographic.nationalgeographic.com

Oxford Ancestors
http://www.oxfordancestors.com/component/option,com_frontpage/Itemid,1

Note: Several laboratories in India, Pakistan, and Bangladesh conduct DNA tests but mostly for forensic, medical, and research purposes. DNA tests for ancestry are usually done with saliva that is collected painlessly from the mouth. Attempts were made to determine if such tests for individuals are available at these laboratories but the responses were not affirmative. This may change.

USEFUL WEBSITES

Howard Hughes Medical Institute,
http://www.hhmi.org/biointeractive/using-dna-trace-human-migration

Institute of Human Origins, Arizona State University, https://iho.asu.edu

National Geographic Genographic Project,
https://genographic.nationalgeographic.com

Smithsonian National Museum of History,
http://humanorigins.si.edu/research

INDEX

ABOUT THE AUTHOR

David G. Mahal is the founder and president of DGM Associates, a business services and communications firm. Before starting DGM Associates, he held management positions at several multinational companies, including Air India, Xerox Corporation, and a Howard Hughes organization. His multifaceted career includes roles as a management consultant, software developer, instructor, author, and publisher. David published a journal on technology for fifteen years, and is the author of the book *Before India: Exploring Your Ancestry with DNA*. He earned the advanced executive MBA from the Peter Drucker School of Management at Claremont Graduate University, an MS from the University of Rochester, and a BA from Dominican College. He is an instructor in business management at the University of California, Los Angeles (UCLA).

Made in United States
Orlando, FL
18 December 2022

27080824R00095